MY OWN
BACKYARD

First published 1994 by WOLFHOUND PRESS Ltd
68 Mountjoy Square
Dublin 1
Ireland

British Library Cataloguing-in-Publication Data
A catalogue record for this book is available from the British Library

ISBN 0 86327 461 7

Wolfhound Press receives financial assistance from the Arts Council/An Chomhairle Ealaíon, Dublin, Ireland.

Cover: Daire Ní Bhréartúin
Typesetting: Wolfhound Press
Printed in Ireland by Betaprint.

Cover photographs: Cecil Sheridan, Danny Cummins, Mickser Reed and Noel Purcell play-acting outside the Savoy, c1950, courtesy of Mrs M Coleman; Guinness barge loaded with empties returning to brewery, 1947, courtesy of Guinness Ireland Ltd; Children playing, courtesy of Bord Fáilte.

CONTENTS

INTRODUCTION

My *Own Backyard* is the story of a young boy growing up in the fifties. It could have been the story of any young boy growing up in Crumlin, however, it was yours truly.

I grew up on the Drive in Crumlin – leastways, we referred to the Drive as being in Crumlin, but the real address was Kimmage. We never used the real address though 'cause my Da objected to the song 'Three Lovely Lassies from Kimmage'.

My Own Backyard tells my kids where their oul' fellah came from, and how far he'll travel for his when need be. Law of God and man aside until after survival.

The reason for the work is that I got sick and tired saying no to my kids whenever they wanted to get up to a bit of divilment. Saying no but knowin' full well in me heart and soul I wouldn't a even thought o' askin' as a young fellah. Just have done it and put up with the consequences.

This book shows how free we were as children, and the values of the times. Money was either good or bad, and the same title applied to its owner. Bad money owners could never command respect. A simple moral code but effective. Money hard earned was to be respected. Wasn't it lovely to have an oul' wan shoutin' in a shop, 'I'll not spend my man's hard-earned money on that dirt.' If her oul' lad worked on the bins for the Corpo, no odds, that family's money was spotless.

The message to me as a kid was clear – if you mixed good and bad money, you only ended up with the sum total in bad money. The same for people, 'Tell me who you go with and I'll tell you what you are.'

I hope those who read this will get the smell of the fifties, when a German was a Kraut and *swinehund* the only word he said, and 'made in Japan' was a label that belonged on any oul' clap-trap that was banjaxed or would be shortly.

The writer is glad to report that all me three children follow in their mother's footsteps so far. A real touch of class she is. Born, bred and reared it, and passin' it on to ours. God smiled on me there, while the divil blinked. Good stock that knows how to win. In short, a lady.

The odd time there's a nark in the house nowadays, and it goes to a vote whether I'm to clear out. I suspect it's the pocket money that's really bein' voted on, and I always manage to scrape on with the title of Our Da.

Many thanks to Michael Davitt, Rebecca Wilkinson, Peter Walsh, Larry Dempsey, Brian Dennis, without their support this work would have remained the great unfinished.

Greg Dalton

EARLY DAYS

My early memories of the Drive in Crumlin are about our home itself. A three-bedroomed terraced house, clean as a whistle, the smell of lavendar polish. The Ma workin' away, cleanin' out the ashes from the fire daily. The two sisters watchin' on an' the two brothers doin' the same. They're all older then me so I just followed in their footsteps. There was always loads goin' on in our house. Outside was the Drive, all three hundred houses the same, we knew nearly all by name, and whether worker or idler.

Travellin' salesmen thought our road was a must, and not a day went by without one callin'. How in the name o' Jasus did they get so much stuff into their cases? Let one o' them get a foot in the door and you were buckled.

If the Ma had slipped up and bought something from one of the salesmen, when Da came home from work she'd make a special fuss of him before she'd show him the new miracle purchase. If he blew a fuse and started her crying, she'd go on about her children in heaven and work on the sympathy bit. Da'd listen for a while and then comfort her.

This nearly always worked except for the day she bought the vacuum cleaner. 'What sort of a fuckin' idiot do you take me for?'

Da wanted to know. 'A vacuum cleaner and no effin' carpets!'

The Ma said it'd do away with all the dustin', but Da said she'd be like Tarzan's Jane with all the muscles she'd develop using that contraption to strangle herself with instead of a cloth. She just ignored him an' said she'd need it for the Venetian blinds she was gettin'.

'What Venetian blinds? Why not just move to Italy?' says Da. Next the tears came and the bit about the brothers and sisters who didn't survive birth.

The Da had had enough so he asked her, 'Who made the coffins, dug the holes and brought the little angels in their coffins on his bike to bury them?' This time he cried and she comforted him sayin' the good Lord giveth and the good Lord taketh away. When the Venetian blinds came there was no row.

But what next but Uncle Joe 'the painter' had to come to paint the house inside and out. Jasus, the colours, all mixes he'd left over from other jobs. Da said the house was like a rainbow and Joe got the pot o' fucking gold. I told Da I thought it was brilliant and Da told me if I had a thought I'd be dangerous.

Lucky for all of us there were a few disasters in the Northside soon after that changed the drift o' things. An unexploded bomb dropped by the Germans was found in the Tolka river and, shortly after, a week's downpour of rain along with a hightide flooded Fairview. We had relations there so Da had to go over and give a dig out. Work always shut him up and the Ma made sure he was always busy.

Da had a simple view on life: protect, clothe, feed and keep warm – that was his duty. Ma had 'notions', as he put it, but he dealt with them in his own way. Like the time she bought candlewick bedspreads and winter sheets, he still threw his Crombie coat on the bed every night. It was his statement that he was the boss. We knew different and Ma just let him do it.

I often crept into their bed after he'd gone to work and wrapped meself in the Crombie and wondered would I ever get to fill one just like his. The smell o' Da riddled through the overcoat and when he wore it he was like a filmstar.

Ma and Da were real tight behind all the talk. When he got sick and the doctor called an ambulance to bring him to hospital there was an uproar. We couldn't believe it, Da sick and two ambulance men bringin' him downstairs on a stretcher! The ambulance men were really flummoxed when they got him down to the hall and Ma stood at the door and wouldn't let them take him out feet first. Da was in bits trying to pass kidney stones and asked her to forget her superstitions just for one day. Ma'd have none of it and told him he'd thank her later even though he was bein' put out.

She got her way and Da used to say after that's why he married her. He'd say, 'Your Ma'll always say the way things are and not the way she'd like them to be, and that's what a man wants.'

Facts were facts to Ma. A few oul' wans who had worked as whores lived on the road. They nearly lived in the church, if they weren't in the church they'd be callin' to the priests' house or goin' to Lough Derg. The Ma just ignored them and used to say, 'There's none so pure as a reformed whore.' I thought they must have been next to saints because I didn't know what a whore was.

I was only the nipper in the gaff and didn't really know the background to a lot of the dealings that went on, they started long before I was born. My job was to fit in and be loyal to mine.

Da was big on loyalty and told me its value often enough. The bottom line to him was: 'A coward dies a thousand deaths, a brave man only one.' Then he'd give me an explanation: 'No one is afraid o' bein' dead,' he'd say, 'it's the dyin' bit that makes the coward. God has it written in the sky how each of us is goin' to go so why back off? You may as well meet him goin' forward as backward.'

Da may have understood this, but this nipper didn't.

WHAT WAS AROUND US

As most of the families who lived in Crumlin were from the inner city we had a sense of relationship with each other. In my case the Da came from Patrick Street and the Ma from the Tenters. This resulted in me knowin' where I fitted in in my backyard – the city – with the boul' Nelson on his Pillar smack on in the middle. No matter where I went I'd meet someone who knew the oul' wan or oul' fellah. Jasus, I was only sorry they knew who I was most of the time. Nothin' worse than some git shoutin' at ya, 'I'll see your father in the job on Monday and we'll see how smart you are then, son. And him so respectable with his big job in Guinness's.' Fuck them.

On the other hand families knowin' families meant that we were safe even when we were up to some divilment. The chances were if the worst came to the worst and you got nabbed, the person who caught you either knew you or yours. So no big deal, just accept the clatter and shut up and hope the git who caught you did the same. It really depended on how well you or your family were known to tell how much you could get away with.

Problems only really raised their head when one hand didn't know what the other hand was doin'. If one end of the family took a stand on something it was up to them to let the rest of the relations know what they were doing. If they didn't and any of the clan came a cropper, whoever took the stand had some explainin' to do. This could be something simple like not buying coal from a certain coalman who we were dealing with, or more complicated like giving an address of someone which led to grief for them or theirs.

This was where the code of silence came in. If it was a small mistake then the code was evoked in its simple form 'not to be spoken to'. If the clanger was bigger then 'not to be trusted or dealt with'. A big wrongdoin' resulted in not getting the protection of the relations until the spouses that be – uncles, aunts, mothers and fathers – said so. Harsh, but it worked.

Sadly, the worst form of the code was when someone outside the old Dublin families got into grief. Maybe an eviction with repossession and the sheriff involved. You could talk to them about anything except their problem. No safe harbour for them, but it let you see the metal in their clan. Only if they had no relations could they look for support, otherwise you'd only be insulting their lot and askin' for grief.

NEIGHBOURS

As with everything else in this world, there's neighbours and there's neighbours. I had me doubts about many o' them as I'm sure they did about me. But, Jasus, there was one family I'd never understand – the Hudsons. Now the Hudsons were as straight as a die, they even walked that way. To make matters worse they had a pet jackdaw, Percy. Percy had a fondness for me and flew to me whenever I'd be out in the backyard. Naturally I fed him bits of bread and I'd dig up a few worms for him while he'd perch on my shoulder. This bird had a reputation for bein' a bit of a divil, swiping anything shiny and bringing it home to his cage.

Now in the fifties the women took off all their jewellery when they were washin' and they'd leave it on the window sill. Sure if Percy was around, it was gone in a flash and back to his cage. No sooner would he be home then out'd come Mrs Hudson to return the stolen goods. Mrs Hudson knew every ring on the road. No one complained about Percy and sure if a ring didn't show up today, it'd show up tomorrow, no panic.

Percy had a style about him and even put my cat, Tiger, in her place a few times. Poor Tiger, full sure of herself, launching at Percy only to be battered with the wings. Then picked to bejasus before she'd get sense and back off. I reckoned when I'd grow up I'd keep jackdaws – fuck pigeons – and I'd be a millionaire in no time.

Percy passed on, and I grew up, but I still hold on to the memory. Maybe some day I'll fill a loft full of Percys and do things slightly different to the Hudsons! Finders keepers, losers weepers.

Secrets were part and parcel of everyday life. We could hear every word of their rows and they ours through the walls. No one ever passed comment. The Da said Kellys were the same as us and entitled to their privacy. Jasus, oul' man Kelly and his missus were forever shoutin' at one another.

The Kellys were bookmakers and owner-trainers and kept numerous greyhounds which from time to time jumped into our back garden. This would delight our dog, Flossy, but caused consternation in our house. Ten dogs in a twenty by ten square yard garden, all excited, and little oul' Dolly Kelly shouting over the hedge, 'They'll do you no harm. Don't move.' And so the parade of dogs started through our house back into Kellys' one by one.

During the day the procession of walking the dogs was the main event. If Jimmy, the Kellys' dog walker, was on the beat, the dogs got no further than the plots where the new church, St Bernadette's, stands on the Drive. They'd be carefully tied to the railings while he went into Flood's pub. The inevitable always happened. A dog would break loose and total chaos would ensue with Jimmy running up and down the street to catch the hound. Needless to say, the dog knew what was coming when he was caught and it took four or five men to corner him. Jimmy would then kick the living daylights out of the animal and drag all the dogs home after two hundred yards exercise.

To get results Jimmy resorted to other tactics – anything so long as the dogs weren't walked. Before a race a diet of porter laced with raw eggs would be administered – by Dolly, otherwise Jimmy would scolp the lot. Then on the day of the race the dog would be blooded or given a kill. This was usually done in the coal shed. The dog was thrown in a live rabbit to kill. If a rabbit was not to be had in the petshop a cat with his claws taped would make the same difference. All this was done in a very reverend manner which seemed to say, 'Don't ask any questions or you don't belong!'

I made it clear to Jimmy that if anything happened to my cat, Tiger, I'd spike all ten dogs by putting DDT in their food. From that point on I was the enemy. My Da heard of my declaration and I got a hidin' for talking like that to a grown man. I think he was a bit wary of me as I made it clear that my cat came first and fuck Kellys. I was then outside the code of silence and in' Coventry'. This really meant that I was fair game for the brothers and sisters. They did no different to me and gave me a dog's life.

While you might think the dogs caused friction, they actually had the opposite effect. We had an understanding with that family and in a way we were one family. I could eat in there or at home the same as any of them and the only time we were really sorted out was at bed time as the small houses had no spare rooms.

Rejoice! Rejoice! Old Charlie died and the Kellys had to move. Why in the name of Jasus was Dolly crying? Didn't she get what she wanted? That oul' wan must have been mad all along and oul' Charlie right. I pointed this out to Da and he says, 'That's what women are like, son. Don't ever count on one or you're asking for trouble.'

Out went the Kellys and in came the Thompsons. This house

on our left-hand side didn't seem to be too lucky because old man Thompson only got two years and then he snuffed it. Me eldest brother, Freddie, who was an absolute authority on nothin' other than bad language, came up with the notion that the dogs had something. My suspicion was that it was all down to the coal shed, and that exorcism – whatever that was – was needed.

Would you believe it? The priests bought the house and in they moved. We were all a bit nervous then. The Ten Commandments gettin' too close. Now maybe they'd seep through the wall. A year or two went by and who did we get but the Reverend Father Michael Clery, the publican's son from Blanchardstown, and before you know it what did he get but a fucking boxer dog called Billy. Billy took a lump out of me and I carry the scar to this day. At the time the Very Reverend had to prove it was an accident. Not my imagination and me mistaken. Can you believe it? I was the bait. He called me over and there was the boul' Billy walking around the yard. Over the boxer strolled and as cool as you like, no warning, had another go at me. This time I moved like greased lightning and into my own house. 'See, Father? No lies.'

Mind you, I had a fondness for Billy, with him on my side I could have taken on all of Crumlin. As it was I'd have to settle for the Drive.

MOULDING YOUNG MINDS

School was bad enough with seventy odd of us in the one class. I'll never forget the first day. Six years old. Being tested to see how much I knew and where I'd fit in. Me Ma sneaking off, me doin' the hard shaw, no tears here – too big an audience. I cried inside though and to put the cap on it, I was accused of copying by the teacher. The spitting image of me granny she was and just as ancient. But there were some right gobshites in my class of 1956. One thing was for sure I wouldn't have to work too hard at lessons to stay out of harm's way.

For us the way to better ourselves was decided by the Church in Dáil Éireann. (No politician had a prayer of gettin' into Dáil Éireann without a priest standing beside him when he was on the soapbox.) Education was the key to the future. The three so-called Rs: Reading, Writing and Arithmetic. Little wonder we were confused when at six years of age we were introduced to poetic licence straight off!

University? Sure that was for the Parish Priest's nephews and nieces, if it stopped there. The truth of the matter was we knew we'd be let go so far but no further. Me granny came up with the answer as always: 'The teacher will teach you but the world will educate you.' Some consolation when we were being introduced to the cane or leather strap just puttin' up with the teachin'. Good Jesus, what was goin' to happen when it came to the world educatin' us?

How in the name o' Jasus did they pick the Irish teachers though? All dedicated to showing us how ignorant we were and taking delight in punishing us for our ignorance. They knew well the power of the Irish over us. Without it no government job and so it made them gods, nearly on a par with the bishops.

Now and then a teacher of the native tongue got carried away with giving one of us a right hiding. The only way to sort him out'd be to get me big brother Gussie to introduce him to Crumlin, formal like. Just tell the brother the facts and show the wheel marks on me hands, arse or legs. Next day or so the brother'd call down and politely ask *An Múinteoir* what part of the country he came from and was it far. Next suggest that the one hundred and fifty miles or so he'd come to teach'd be nothin' to the one hundred and fifty yards or so he'd be kicked comin' or goin' to class if he didn't change his ways *go* fucking *tapaigh*.

This worked in one sense as at least you'd be safe, but you'd be taught fuck-all Irish. The brother went a bit far with one *Múinteoir* who wrote my oul' fellah complaining. Now had the *Múinteoir* the savvy and waited till the marks from the hiding he gave me cleared up, the git would have got away with it. But my luck was in and off with me, the brod and the oul' fellah. The smile on the git's face as he held his hand out to the Da! You'd think he was going to give the Da a bleedin' gold *fáinne*.

Now the Da was particular about who he shook hands with, so he just ignored it. No fuss, steps beside *An Múinteoir*. Next he pulls out the note written in English and asks the *Múinteoir* to explain. Not another word out of the Da.

Now *An Múinteoir* is beginning to feel a little uncomfortable, definitely not one of Sarsfield's ten men. Bleedin' yellow with a red neck and face, not a 'fuckal' out of *An Múinteoir*.

The Da, breaking the silence, had real style and explains that if *An Múinteoir* lays a hand on me again, the brother will get the worst hiding of his life from Da. 'Next you'll be on the agenda for me,' the Da says to Fionn Mac Cumhaill's would-be descendant. 'I'll allow you decide whether you want the hiding I'll give you in the grounds of the Guards Barracks or the Hospital, whichever suits you. As a matter of fact, to be expedient and economic with time, perhaps you should chose now and that way we'll all know where we stand.'

The Da turns to the brod then. 'Did you hear what I said, son?' and he looked at Gussie eye to eye. The brod nodded, but that's not good enough for Da who shouts, 'I can't hear you, son!' And the brod shouts back 'Yes!' Then Da looks at the gutless Gael, and back at the brother and says, 'Believe you me, I'm not askin' you to do much.'

Off with us back home and although me *Múinteoir* didn't get a hiding, I'm happy enough. To see him squirm like the villain in the folly 'n' upper flicks on a Saturday in the Bower cinema at the top of the Drive! (The last thing any kid wanted was to be sick on a Saturday, and missing the folly 'n' uppers. That'd mean missing the start of a new film, the end of an old one and the middle of the one you'd seen started last week.) All the Gael's power didn't add up to much punch in the man department. And as for teachin'! We knew who was educatin' who. The only word I spoke to him after that was *Anseo* ('present'), and Jasus knows he came terrible close to getting his.

To No Man's Land

E ven though we'd got off to a bad start with the Irish the oul'
lad wouldn't let go of it. The Gaeltacht was his answer. Six
weeks in Gortahork for ten pounds. Sure I thought I was being
adopted. Me summer holidays gone and me havin' no say at all.
The Da was delighted with it and wanted to know why he hadn't
been told about it years ago.

Gaeltacht he wanted, Gaeltacht I got. Dublin to Belfast by
train and then bus to Donegal. Now the gang of us from school
arrived at the cottage we were to stay in. Christ Almighty, straw
roof and lashings o' rain. Sure we'll never see Dublin again,
bound to get TB out o' this dive.

Introductions all around. I may as well've been on Mars, not
knowin' a word of what was bein' said. However the *Bean an Tí*
takes six of us in, shows us to our room. Three bunk beds in a
boxroom, at least we'd be together. Then she calls us out to eat. She
introduces herself informally along with the da and grandad.

I couldn't take me eyes off the fireplace – it took up the whole
wall. Curiosity got the better of me and I had to ask about it in
English. Fair dues to the oul' wan, she explained about the two
seats in inside the fireplace. Then she allows us speak English
while we settle down. No complaints so far.

Next the grub. Never ate a meal as good before or since. Bacon, cabbage and spuds. First she put the cabbage on the plates, then a piece of bacon. Over she strolls with her apron full o' spuds and plops the lot on to the centre of the table. There must o' been a half stone of spuds. Flowery with the skins just burstin'. I ate eight or ten before I realised everyone else was peeling them. A big dollop of butter and a drop o' milk. Jasus, I'd sleep tonight. No brothers or sisters robbin' off me plate. Then, after I'm full, the *Bean an Tí* puts an apple tart on the table. If she keeps this up I'm stayin'. A full gut, the smell of the turf burnin', small wonder they're in bad humour leavin' this behind to come to Dublin to teach us the Irish. They have it made.

Naturally we ask why there's doors on each side o' the house and she explains that's because of the wind. If the wind blows one way you come in the other door. A real gem. Then she shows me the coffin bed the oul' granda sleeps in, like a big tea chest. I'd no time to be homesick with all I was learnin'.

These were beautiful people, simple and kind, easygoin', no fuss, just live and enjoy God's goodness. To put us at ease the lady told us a story of a shipwreck just six weeks before and promised to bring us down to the wreck. We were in heaven and I tell the *Bean an Tí*. She takes a shinin' to me.

Within a few days I'm feedin' the chickens and milkin' the cows and then off to school. The mates thought I'd gone soft but here was somethin' special. The *Fear an Tí* used to laugh at me – a Jackeen, completely at home. Sure I had to tell him that when we called someone a culchie or redneck in Dublin it really went against the grain. Most of our grandparents had come to Dublin from the country, so it wasn't really an insult. He broke his sides laughin' when I went out with me shovel to save the cow manure for the *Bean an Tí*'s flowers. Then I told him how valuable it was in Dublin. He was kind of sad at what the city was doin' to us and told me Gaeltacht or not, ten pounds or not, if I ever wanted a place to come to, come to him and I knew he meant it. His *céad míle fáilte* was true blue.

Just to walk out either door of the house and look over at Chnoc Folla (Bloody Foreland Mountain) and even get to climb it! Another day over to Devil's Hole, a blow hole, to hear the roar as the water gushed in and burst up into the air. It didn't matter if we got wet, sure we'd dry off sooner or later. The *céilí* twice a week was a must. Legs goin' this way and that way as we laughed at ourselves.

Goin' to school was an adventure in itself. If we went by the bog-road it was a two mile walk, as the crow flies no more than a half mile. Mind you, there were two streams to be crossed by stepping stones. Someone always ended up in the drink with our messin'. Had this happened back in Crumlin there would've been a war. Here we just laughed, even meself at meself when I was pushed in.

It couldn't last and it didn't, eventually we had to head home. Irish had a new meaning for me: it was in the heart. Small wonder the teachers were frustrated in Crumlin, sure the cart was before the horse. Why couldn't we have had the Gaeltacht first and the lessons after? One thing for sure, I learned my Irish from then on and took pride in it.

Many's the time later on in life and overseas in a strange city, someone would hear my accent, then walk over and say, '*Conas atá tú, a chara?*' It's only when it happens you know the feeling of being Irish. The smells well up inside you, the sight of the men shearing sheep, the women with the spinning wheels working away outdoors on a fine day, the *currachs* high up on the beaches upside-down never leaves you.

On the journey back home I started to look at what I was going home to. Being one up was what it was all about at home. It came to me as naturally as everybody else. Knowing the facts was simple enough. How to survive with the least bother was the hard bit.

Going back to the Ma gettin' in the messages twice a day. The two ounce packets of tea, the sevenpenny brown paper bag of sugar, or the quarter pound of butter. The Gaeltacht wouldn't change much for her.

She had no cows for milk or butter, no bog for fuel, just that little brown wore-out purse. That purse was her store – why wouldn't she mind every copper in it?

I was proud to stand beside her when she'd bargain down a shopkeeper. Not at all shy like I used to be. 'Money hard earned should be hard spent,' was her sayin' and doin'.

For the few years that followed I'd often walk up to the hardware shop at the top of the Drive just to feel part of Gorta-hork again. Just to look around the shop, and see the spades and forks, seed potatoes and plants, or maybe even a *sleán* for cutting turf. Gone but not forgotten.

A LITTLE BIT OF HEAVEN

Up until the time I was seven, Mass was neither here nor there. God lived in the church and seemed happy enough to stay there. I was certainly happy with that deal. Who in their right mind'd want to sign up to goin' to Confession and Mass every week?

The Ma decides to explain the need for religion to me. She tells me I'll never walk alone after me First Holy Communion. Jasus, that's all right providin' God keeps his mouth shut on what's goin' on, is goin' through my mind. Comfort or threat, I don't know, still don't!

If all this God stuff is so great, I'd be thinkin', why aren't all the clergy like the Japanese Zero pilots, committin' suicide to join him in Valhalla? Do they think I'm stupid? I've learned all I want to know about purgatory, limbo, hell and heaven, but no matter what I think, one way or the other I'm goin' to be enlisted.

They were building a basilica down at the plots on the Drive. A new church. Sure what was wrong with the old one? We were told it was too small to serve the community and that was true enough. At Mass on Sunday we were like sardines in a tin. Wouldn't it make sense though if you could get Mass on any day instead of a Sunday only? That way, sure, it would do fine.

Freddie said it was all because of the Jews. 'We have to show them we're better and bigger than them.' The thinking was that they did bugger all on the Sabbath or Saturday. As our big day was Sunday, it'd be was easy to put a better show on. Besides that, since Jesus started out life as a Jew we were kind of obligated to show some progress.

Well now, when the brother said Jesus was a Jew, I said sweet fuck-all as I knew he was mad. In my Catechism it said clearly that the Jews killed Christ. What way was it put? 'The Roman Governor, Pontius Pilate, killed Christ at the behest of the Jews.' I made my mind up not to put much store in any information from the Absolute Authority any-fucking-more.

What we thought made no difference, and the church went ahead anyway. My suspicion was that it was all over the Parish Priest's bees. We'd been catching those bees in the plots for years and he'd been giving out fuck about it as long, even from the pulpit. What did he want those hives for? If anyone could afford to buy a jar of honey it was him. The oul' fellah said, 'Pay the oul' PP no heed. It's really Father Rhattigan who's in charge,' he bein' the PP's left and right hands. That made sense, he fitted the bill, Kerry blue dogs and all.

Well, the church finally got under way and, lo and behold, it was a goldmine. All the timber we could ever want, all the nails we'd ever want. Sure it was a little bit of heaven already. We had the best of huts and gigs and pigeon lofts in all Dublin without a doubt.

The clergy didn't see it like that, it was plain oul' stealing and we were all damned. Every Sunday up there in the pulpit. Them saying they knew the houses to call to and who was responsible, and restitution would have to be made.

The Absolute Authority wanted to know who was paying

anyway. He had no intention of returning his now full pigeon loft. How in the name o' Jasus could you rob yourself? he wanted to know. But somehow or other his voice was lost as he wasn't exactly shouting it back at the pulpit. Made sense enough to me and the mates though. No way were we closing down our goldmine. But things got nasty, especially when the lead and copper appeared.

At first we wanted the lead to make heads for our arrows, or weights for fishing, and took the copper because it was nice and shiny. We just wanted it. Sure we thought it was near gold. Then when we found out that we could sell it, well, you can imagine yourself. Jasus, there was a trail worn out on the path to the scrapman. Next, we got a warning from the pulpit and we were all frying in hell. Sure we'd spent the money, and now we were being threatened with 'the Force'. Sweet Jesus, couldn't they see that the only way we could make restitution was to rob more? That was if the restitution notion took us at all.

The lure of the shilling was proving too much. Next there were day watchmen, night watchmen, and watchmen watching watchmen. Now a watchman in Crumlin had to be a bad joke. Well, now they were challenging us! We'd see who was watching what, Reverends. The dander was up, and from here on in with the outsider watchmen, whatever conscience we'd had up until now was gone altogether.

The best way to get whatever we wanted was out the main gates of the site and that was the way it came. Just brazen it out. Now, you can only eat so many sweets and drink so much lemonade, so as the church was nearing completion, we were losing interest, and things were coming back to normal with the clergy. At least we could walk on the same side of the street without the hair standin' up on the backs of our necks.

The inside of the church was decked out behind closed doors. There was a sort of excitement growing now. 'What would it be like?' Some said Lourdes, others Rome, and the brother, Crumlin. In a way it was a miracle the bleedin' thing got finished at all when you look at the disadvantages it was up against. However, finished it was. St Bernadette's.

The first time I walked in, I remember well, with the Ma. 'How in the name o' Jesus are they going to heat this?' she wanted to know. She was right too! The very best of gear everywhere. We were looking in the confessionals and they even had cushions to kneel on. Up in the gods for the choir, the organ and all was first class.

The only thing left to do was pick your seat and scratch your name in it for the generations to come. This I did with great reverence and called me Ma over to see where she wanted her name scratched. Well, I was bet home and told if she ever caught me in there again on me own I'd get more of the same. To put things right she went over to the chemist's and got a bottle of iodine and went back and washed it over me scratches. They could still be seen so she came home and off again with dark brown polish. Jasus help whoever sat there the next Sunday.

A few of the mates saw the handiwork and, mind you, the Mother's formula gave it a kind of upper class status. So I was now the authority on making your mark. Wouldn't you know it, the next Sunday we were vandals, idle hands, and damned again. Eff them! You couldn't win. Who was this bleedin' church for, them or us, or the both?

Now it was a saying in the fifties that when you walked into a church for the first time you got a wish. This was frowned on by the clergy but not really mouthed by them. This was as much as I got done on my first day in there, before I was bet out. What did I spot but candles galore all over the place, just asking to be took? 'God never closes one door before he opens another,' as Granny'd say.

Thanks be to Christ me Ma didn't get her wish or I'd have gone up in a puff of smoke there and then, and I'm sure me oul' fellah wouldn't have been too happy about her implication that maybe I'd no oul' fellah at all, well, leastways not Da. This played on my mind so I asked the brother, and to make matters worse he says: 'Of course you were adopted, but you were sent fucking back.' Thank you, Gussie, I'll never forget your kindness. You never missed out on the opportunity of making a bad situation worse.

Normality in the church was the usual crowd of movin' statue witnesses, left alone they'd have worked on another immaculate conception. The clergy'd knock them on the head, sooner rather than later, to save the faithful from the pitiful.

The next move the religious made was that the Marist nuns decided to build a convent. Where do you think? Smack across the road from Flood's pub. It seemed a bit like Daniel going back into the lions' den to get his cap. At the back of their site was the old dump. Mind you, we left the nuns alone. Sure we had all we wanted from the church and besides we look on them as kind of *real* religious.

PENANCE AND EUCHARIST

The First Holy Communion snuck up on me. It started with penance. All sittin' there in the church waitin' for the priest to come in. At seven years of age we had the guilt of the world on our shoulders. Would we get the big confession right? I thought to meself I'd be better off tellin' what I'd done right, that way it'd be quicker, but the priest insisted on doin' it his way. We all got a practice run anyway. Bein' told it was all right to make up a few yarns just to get comfortable with talkin' in the box. Jasus, that confession box looked and felt like a coffin. The good bit was if you were real quiet. Then you could hear every word that was bein' said by the other eejit on the far side. Now only the priest was duty bound to silence. You can figure out yourself what this led to.

The brother decided I was making a right joke of it so he decides to sort me out. Up he goes to the wardrobe in the bedroom and makes me go through the routine with him dressed up in a white sheet. Like a fool I fall for it and a few of the mysteries of our house are solved. Jasus, Gussie's always one ahead of me. Some day I'll learn.

Now it comes to the real confession and in I go. Fed up. After the formalities I tell the priest, 'I have nothin' to say as the last time I was with you, Father, I told a pack of make-up lies. Then when me brother took charge it ended up with me in right shite.'

Better for the both of us if we leave things as they are. When he worms out of me what I told the brother he can't stop laughin' and I'm scared to leave the bleedin' box. I've forgotten to whisper so the world an' his wife know my mortallers. When he asks me about bad language, no better man, so I give him a demonstration as requested. The laugh goes to the other side of his face, I should've brought the brother – same as the *Múinteoir*, you hurt me, the brother hurts you. How an' ever it was too bleedin' late. As a last gasp I throw in that the divil looks after his own anyway so it doesn't matter which way I go. Didn't work.

I got ten Our Fathers and ten Hail Marys for me trouble. The worst part was on me way out he tells me to tell me Ma he was askin' for her and says, 'How are her varicose veins?' Buckled again! Jasus, I earned me Communion money the hard way.

Da's job – controlling the uncontrollable. *Above:* The cooperage yard at St James's Gate Brewery, 1956. 250,000 barrels could be seen there any day.

Right and overleaf: The Guinness Planet Diesel Locomotive at the Victoria Quay Jetty, 1958. (Photos courtesy of Guinness Ireland Ltd)

Seeing all these barrels, let me tell you something about this romantic trade of the coopers. Firstly, this trade of making casks was handed from father to son. After serving six or seven years cutting staves and belting hoops, the cooper made his first barrel. Some took great pride in this work, more wished to Jasus they'd never heard of a stave as the old craftsmen didn't mind where they hit an apprentice with one when they'd made a mistake. Who could they complain to if it was their own ol' man or uncle hit them? If you want to know the truth, ask any cooper. They were delighted to see the new stainless steel casks, and not as worried as your man in the song at all. No, it was a happy release for them, except for the few usual diehards, you know yourself.

Nelson's Pillar, O'Connell Street, 1955. Didn't matter to us who was up there. (Photo courtesy of Guinness Ireland Ltd)

Cuffe Street in the late 1950s. The only pawnshop that dealt in false teeth – but they had to be the full set. (Photo courtesy of Mrs M. Coleman)

The National Stadium in South Circular Road was the only place to box in Dublin. Could break your heart as well as your nose.

Great fun – 'til you banged your head on the pole! (Courtesy of Bord Fáilte)

The Inkblots v The Crackpots – a regular Dublin charity fundraiser. The four Daddies of Dublin *(from right)* Cecil Sheridan, Noel Purcell, Danny Cummins and Mickser Read. (From a glass positive courtesy of Mrs M. Coleman).

The heart of Dublin, O'Connell Bridge. To dodge the photographers here as you crossed over was an art in itself. (Photo courtesy of Guinness Ireland Ltd)

The author, born, bred and reared in Dublin.

Centre: The old church on Clogher Road where I was christened.

Bottom: The Barracks, every drunkard's nightmare. When caught, the key to success was and is to get all matters *sub judice* (below justice). A lovely way of saying 'We'll use the courts to put the people of Ireland in coventry or wonderland.' The law has become a jinnet. How many notaries dried out in clinics over the weekend to decide on our future the following Monday? Those who can't run their own houses and are barred from them, are running the country and trying to manage the last thirty pieces of silver until they get the next ones. A cuteness beyond all cuteness. Whether they came to praise Caesar or bury him was down to shillings. Judas' downfall was that he wasn't Irish.

My 'guardian angel', Gussie, gets his medal and cert from Ben Briscoe, Lord Mayor of Dublin, in 1956 for pulling a young fella out of the canal at Sally's Bridge (see below).

Centre: The new church from Sundrive Road. We're a real miracle nation all right. If they rob or conspire behind a closed door, even when found out nothing happens. Plenary indulgences all round by directors of no prosecution. Sure Jesus Christ would have been proud of these miracles. Can you imagine the consternation the boul' Jesus would have caused the Roman Emperor had he been from the Emerald Isle?

I never got a free
biscuit out of
Jacobs, and I never
got a free swim in
the Iveagh; but
Jacobs' horses
manured the
garden and
learning to swim in
the Iveagh Baths
saved my life.

SCRAPPIN'

Trouble always seemed to follow me about. Sure I was wore out scrappin' from me earliest moment. Every bloke I hit always got a black eye or a bloody nose. One dig i'd do it. In school I was in a class of thirty-five boys and thirty-five girls and expected to stay out of trouble. I ask ya? I spent more time in the corner facing the wall than anywhere else in the classroom. I could o' rented out my place. 'Live horse, eat grass'– let them sort the pecking order out. That way I'd only be in trouble the once. But while the peckin' order was being sorted out I made friends with most.

The gurrier who made it to the top of the heap was Dermot Casey. A clear three inches taller than me, and only me left to master and then he was the Boss. Sure I'd a sooner left him the Boss than tangle with him. He talked kinda funny, country like, his knuckles looked like four gulliers on each hand, in God's truth I was scared. He pushed and shoved me for a week at least, in between classes, after school, broke me pencils, until finally he trips me up. Well there I was on the wooden floor nearly in tears with all me classmates lookin' on. I knew well it was now or never, if it was now it'd better be fast. Up I gets, sorts meself out as best I can. One dig on his nose did the job, like turning a tap on. But I knew I was in the shit again. Next day his ma's down in the school and me granny's spittin' image gives me a hiding. Makes no odds though – I promise the boul' Dermo the best o' torment for the rest o' his natural.

At six or seven I was quite big for my age and so nine or ten year olds would have a go at me. I told my brother Gussie the problem and he said to get in first and fast whenever I felt outmatched. At least that way I'd do a decent bit of damage even if I did go to hospital. This made sense so I did it the first time I was claimed around in the field at the back of our houses.

Young O'Brien, aged twelve, whose oul' fellah kept horses in the backyard, decided to take me on. He said I was a poshy just 'cause we lived in our own house on the Drive, all paid for. His supporters stood aside, I was on my own. There was no way to win. If I gave him a hiding his mates would kick me to death. My pride was at stake then and I wouldn't back off. Jasus, I put him down ten times but he kept gettin' up, I didn't want to be dirty or I'd have given his mates reason to move on me.

Thanks be to God and His Blessed Mother, who arrived but the brother, Gussie? Now this neutralised O'Brien's mates as the brother could deliver the goods there. Now I was covered, and what did O'Brien do, blood all over his face 'cause he had oul' wan's hands to match his mouth, but pick up a brick and swing at my head? The fool moved so slow he could have written it out for me. I started laughing when he missed me but it got very edgy with the on-lookers. He let the brick slip when I dropped him again. I picked it up and showed it to one and all while I sat on top of him and then the brother said it was time to finish it. So goodbye to O'Brien's nose and front teeth, compliments of his brick. No more bother around that corner anymore. I could stand there waiting on a bus anytime I liked. The word went about and this resulted in all the kids on the road being taken in when I was out. 'He's the same as his brothers,' they'd say. What did they expect? Stupid we weren't!

The code of silence was invoked by all but this time it only half worked. It took a year for my oul' man to find out. Something had happened between the O'Briens and my oul' man at some stage and it suited me Da not to hear. The deaf ear! I was one hundred percent off the hook. Jasus, I hadn't been looking forward to that reckoning.

Now you might think this savage for a kid of six or seven but in its time and place it was perfect justice and neither me nor the brother hung around to see who took O'Brien home that day, but fair dues to him he kept his mouth shut about it, even though a lot of his so-called mates didn't. He knew that I respected his 'bottle' or 'moxie' and I knew that he respected mine.

THE SISTERS

The sisters had a big influence on me. Maisie and Agnes, always full of notions, talk this way, walk this way, smile, and show your teeth. The nuns were doing a great job on them. The Ma thought it was great when they'd pull me up for eating with a knife or dirty hands.

Whenever it came down to simple things like gettin' in a bucket of coal, or running over to the shops for a loaf of bread, no way would they move. It was either 'That's not women's work' or 'A lady shouldn't have to do that.'

'Not women's work', worked for them, and muggins here was always elected. 'A lady shouldn't have to do that' drove me and the oul' fellah mad. 'Is this what I'm payin' those so-and-so nuns for?' he'd say. The Ma always took up for them, 'Now, Da, you know yourself that they're at an awkward age, or that way.' He always backed down. And them sisters standin' there looking down at the floor like butter wouldn't melt in their mouths!

I ask the oul' fellah when I'm going to reach that awkward age 'cause the feet are run off me doin' their work. Me timing wasn't right – just after one of these showdowns – and he lets fly with 'If you ever fuckin' do I'll bury you.' Won't be raisin' that conversation again!

So the sisters have it all their own way, even the brothers walk around them. If I'd've been as big as the brothers I'd've burst them. But the oul' fellah taught them well. 'Only a coward hits a woman.' That's all very fine for the brothers 'cause they'd win, why can't he come up with something like that for me? Those sisters clatter me whenever they like, even when they don't like, just for something to do.

I'm wore out going for nylon stockings, lipstick and fucking nail polish. Just get out and stay out, is the only answer I have so that's what I do. Be goin' somewhere or doing something was the solution. Only then I see the oul' fellah and the brothers are doin' the same for years without tellin' me. Just leave the sisters the whole gaff that way if they fall out it's nothing to do with us, and the Ma has to sort it out. Confession was the day's excuse and going to copy me homework was the night's one.

I can still see them there studying for the exams so they could get good jobs in the bank when they'd done the secretarial courses. Then wait for Prince Charming to come along – a gobshite, in other words. In the meantime they'd have to put nail polish on their nylons to stop them running as the oul' fellah wouldn't let up on the one pair a week. That was the only control either God or man ever had over them.

Mind you their notions took them a long ways with their Prince Charmings. The good Lord seemed to be better to them than most, and I'm still bewildered as much today as I was then by them and their antics.

Clatter me for taking the last slice of bread on the plate inside the house. But outside just like the Ma, touch me and they'd take a bite out of you, if you were lucky. Ah, they were never right, fancy drooling to the sound of Jim Reeves when they coulda been alive with Little Richard. The perfume when you went into their room'd knock you over, not natural deffo. When you walked into our room you always knew who was after changing their socks last by the smell. Even the Ma knew. But in the sisters' room only God knew.

The oul' fellah takes pity on me and decides to have a heart to heart chat with me. He starts out by tellin' me how special the sisters are and it's our job to look after them. They have him wrapped up the same as the Ma. Then he tells me how in time they'll turn out the same as their mother, all girls do. Naturally he's left himself wide open so I ask him, did he see Granny before he got married? Did he see her with her tripe 'n' onions and bleedin' milk stout, 'n' snuff for afters? End of conversation. He just upped and out. Some expert what?

THE FEIS

L ife moves on and the two sisters make mine a misery. Both
the apples of me Da's eyes, couldn't do a thing wrong. Jasus,
they even did elocution no less. What next? I'll tell ya what next
but the younger skin 'n' blister wins a Feis. Then the elder one
takes up acting. Nothing surer but who else is roped in but
meself. The Ma doesn't like the way I speak so off I go to the
Marian Actors with the sisters.

Before I knew it I was entered into a Feis. Mind you, not any
oul' Feis but the *Feis Maitiú*, I'll have you know. The Ma was
delighted at me being picked to do me piece. The sisters were
goin' to coach me, sure all I had to do was show up. I knew that
before any of this guff started, but now I had to do it.

> *I have a little dog*
> *Whose name is Spot*
> *And whether he's white*
> *Or whether he's not*
> *He's still my dog*
> *My dog, Spot.* (By Rodney Bennett)

Well, Gussie had a field day when he heard the news. What
does he do but write his own version of it for me:

I have a little dog
Whose name is Snot
And he has me in the shite
Over in the Father Matthew Hall
And whether I win, or lose, or draw
I'll kick him to death
For all the grief he's caused. (Gussie)

Knowin' the brother's violent tendency I learn his version quick enough but I have trouble with the real one. Then to make a right nancy o' me, the brother brings his mates in to hear yours truly.

Me big day came and I'm number ninety-six. Well, Jasus! If I didn't know me lines by the time I got up I'd never know them. The trouble started with the Ma tellin' me not to be nervous. Nervous o' what? I'd cleave any o' this shower on me worst day. My problem was when I opened me mouth which version was goin' to come out.

Thanks be to God and His Blessed Mother but the right one came. Then when it was all over an' done with, as I thought, twelve of the ninety-six entrants were recalled – some gobshite of an adjudicator. Spot'd have pups an' all by the time we'd get out.

Up again for the second round and still safe with the right version. Then back to the Ma who tells me not to worry if I don't win. You mean to tell me, Ma, all this shame and grief to lose? Came home with gold, and told the Ma the story of the brod's version. Well, she went white as a sheet and no more elocution for me.

Closer to home I realised that the only thing worse than being in a bleedin' Feis for elocution, was winning it, especially if you live in Crumlin. I could hear the jibes – wouldn't I do it meself to some other bloke? God help me but those fucking sisters had a lot to answer for.

INCHING TO DÁIL ÉIREANN

In the fifties it was a strange, simple attitude we had about the politics. We were all fairly certain that we were being sold out or, at best, sold short, but with the Church in there maybe some good would come of it. The city deputies – believe me they'd never make sheriffs in any of the flicks I saw – would depend on soap boxes for speeches, plain porter was the best convincer. The house to house calling was a bit dodgy in those days as too many rows ensued. The posters were splattered everywhere and if you stood still too long you'd get one stuck on yourself.

Undermining or lyin' about the opposition worked, so this was the way forward to the Dáil. The more outlandish the lie, the better it worked. Examples: 'Sure wasn't his cousin roped in with the German spy in Templeogue?' 'Didn't he do a line with your woman who got knocked up? What became of her? You never hear a word about her now that he's going for office. What was her name now?' 'His family never got into any bother when the Tans were about. Makes you wonder!'

Now when it came to election day the Ma and Da went off to vote together. Da used to have to fill out the form for her 'cause she was afraid she'd get it wrong, as she put it. We knew the truth. The Ma had a fear of forms and left to her own was bound to get it wrong and just as well, so the oul' man did the business and there was no grief all around. She'd be full of herself comin' home. Jasus, if her head'd go any higher she'd be off the ground. Blind allegiance to the blind oul' fellah.

The Dáil, what good could you expect out of it? Sure the elected representatives in rural areas were deciding what the people in Crumlin should have. Jasus, the fools couldn't find Crumlin if you gave them a map. Sure their only concern was really 'What's good for me and mine?' Feeble-minded, short-sighted, well-heeled, and fuck the rest of the Irish. 'Sure aren't they the problem? The cheek of the people of Ireland to expect me to do anything for them, sure they're the same as I was and my oul' fellah before me, before I got into this politickin' busi-ness. Now that I'm in, I'm going to make sure nobody else gets in to share the spoils.' You can be sure no politician was around when Granny was pawning her false teeth in the hock-shop.

Up from the five-eighths of Ireland they'd come, genuflecting to the Church. Sure you'd wonder which was the bigger leech. The blind fellah and those who came with him buttered their own bread well first. Some things don't change.

Didn't the schools do a great job on us all the same? Do you remember, 'Are there ten men who will die for Ireland?' Jasus, the last place you'd find them, my dear Patrick, would be Dáil Éireann anytime.

As for the Seven Poet Politicians with their clamations, for us in Crumlin they may as well have been claiming for Timbuktu for all we got. Lord be good to them, grand notions to be prostituted from 1916 to1926 and, by the fifties, Boland's Mill must have been the size of the Phoenix Park with all that was supposed to have been in it.

Sure, when the dust settled around our glorious uprising, and the blind oul' fellah got the big job he was after. What do you think happened next? He looked into the cupboard and it was bleeding bare, not a shilling. Had it not been for Lord Iveagh of Guinness's and a few like him who pre-paid excise duties, the gallant so-called Free State would never have got off its arse. Costello got elected but Dev got the solicitor's wages. Could you just imagine the shit we'd have been in if the Crown had stopped paying the pensions to the enslaved new Republican citizens. Oh yeah! He became a great statesman all right. It must run in the family. I wonder how many redundancies his family have created for Mother Éire since.

The only time I can remember Europe being talked about was either in school at History or Geography, or else when some high flyer went on holidays. Inevitably he'd be spotted in Skerries or Rush and would have to live it down afterwards. We'd laugh when the truth came out and shout out, 'Was that the south of France or Francis Street you were in?'

For the real McCoy, you'd have to sign up with the Dublin Diocesan Pilgrimage to Lourdes. All the hopeless with hopeful families. A money lender's delight. More people were crucified paying for Lourdes than cures ever came from it. Didn't it sound grand though? 'The Bishop left his Palace to go with us, we're all equal,' but he went back to his Palace. It's only nowadays we see that bishops go to more than palaces, and them that hangs around them do as well as them that hangs around the duly elected.

Ah, we've come a long way now from the blind man to the petfood man via Ballymun into Europe. Stardust on their hands like Lady Macbeth, but they still think there's pockets in a shroud.

THE CENTRE OF POLITICS

Flood's public house on the Drive was the centre of politics. There, on bare boards sprinkled with sawdust, the oul' lads'd decide on the future of our nation. The Irish nationalist spirit was alive and kept alive mainly in the pubs. It was normal to hear an out 'n' out Republican quote from Shakespeare, Milton and the Declaration of Independence in the one night to support an argument he was making for a thirty-two county Republic. It didn't matter that the author wasn't of the same persuasion or country. Just the weight of the words counted, and how they were delivered.

Status was very important in any discussion, and respect was given a man based on what he was drinking rather than sayin'. Take for instance Mr Joyce, a Protestant. His drink'd be whiskey and water with a bottle of stout on the side. Mind you, not too many. A great listener, Mr Joyce, but a man of few words. When he spoke about an issue it was only two or three sentences. He always stumped the most of the men with his words of wisdom. Looking back, I can still see him with his impeccable clothes, a calm confident smile, he even used his hands for expression.

At the other end of the scale was oul' Jem. Knew it all, said it all, but it meant eff all. Full of plain porter, the cheapest of the cheapest gargle. Claimed to be an out 'n' out activist in the Republican Army. Sure the poor divil with his gammy leg wouldn't be let on a darts team, let alone into an army. A great man to set up an argument if some stranger was about. More often than not this resulted in the boul' Jemmer being thrown out by the barmen.

The barmen acted like 'the Force' in that pub. The best laundered aprons in Dublin with their shirt sleeves rolled up to the elbows. They'd saunter from table to table picking up the empty glasses and know all by name and drink. How could they see in the dark and not bump into the tables? Yet they did, and wormed their way around the tables, masters of all they surveyed.

To get a laugh every now and then when the men would be discussing employment, someone would shout in, 'You won't see many *fáinnes* on the board of directors of that company.' Normally these employers would be the powerful ones. It took a long number of years for the penny to drop with me on that one. When it did the sound it made was like a peal of thunder. Sweet Jesus, we the Irish were using the Irish language as a weapon against the Irish. It was true about the *fáinne* in the fifties, gold or silver, and it's true today. Look for *fáinnes* on any board of directors and if you see a few token ones, then the control company is overseas, *fáinne*-free, counting the spoils of their repatriated profits.

An' yeah, it took time to understand 'A troubled Lagan trembled beneath the banks of Belfast,' or 'Men may come and men may go but the cause goes on forever.' The Da'd try to explain the quotes. To me it was all down to the porter. Nothin' would happen one way or the other to change our lot. You can't get much wronger than that.

Da'd go over to Flood's the odd time, whenever the notion

took him. All in all about twice a year and no more than two half pint bottles of stout by the neck. He'd insist on gettin' the glass dry as he said it interfered with the head on the stout if the glass was wet. 'Cause he worked in Guinness's no one ever took him to task on this. To see him there hawing on the glass and then polishing it with a spotless hanky was somethin' else. The way he'd pour it with reverence, making sure none of the sediment rose from the bottom of the bottle and spilled out into his glass. As Flood's did their own bottling from hogsheads, the staff'd be waitin' on my oul' fellah's verdict. It was like a seal of approval when he'd say, 'best bottle I've had in a year'.

I used to love goin' over to tell him his dinner was ready, but I had to time when I said it or it'd screw up his ceremony. As soon as he'd see me he'd beam a big smile and call me over as though I was the only thing that mattered in the world. Even though it was against the law for me to be there no one said a word. My Da commanded respect and that was that.

THE FORCE

The local police minded their own business, whatever that was. Four or five families on our road were in 'the Force'. The streets were patrolled twice daily by foot and only if all hell broke out would the Ford Consul appear. All shiny black, you could hear it start up in the station about a half-mile away and it only caught who or what stayed still. However, they were there.

Caught out with no lights on the bike? Wrong addresses and reverence worked, except when the Garda was a neighbour. Then justice was direct. A clatter on the side of the head or a kick up the arse for thinking him stupid, let alone the no lights on your bike. How could they complain about you anyway when you were doing the same as their kids? If you came home and told the story you'd just get more of the same.

Drunk and disorderly was dealt with straight off. Hold him overnight and if his missus still wanted him – no charge. To decide on the drunk bit, the technology of the day was a piece of chalk. Draw a straight line and off you go. There were some quare straight lines drawn by many a copper. An octopus wouldn't make it.

The paperwork always seemed to be the problem for the boys

in blue as no sooner would the ink be dry than they found out that so-and-so was related to so-and-so who knew so-and-so, and sure how could you do anything on him? More confetti came from summonses than court cases.

The problem came when a new man was after promotion and would stick to the letter of the law. Okay, he'd make the case all right but fuck-all else in Crumlin. The 'bad 'un' had either to be promoted or transferred. Many a copper got transferred after a few tactful complaints appeared on his file. To this end a few notable personalities were available, all tax payers. You see, a tax payer was a big shot. Tax bills were sent out at the end of each year and applied to the previous year's earnings. If you earned more than £30 a week you got one. A few civil servants and Gardaí were not charged tax so no one knew how much went into those houses. Well, not without makin' enquiries leastwise. We got one through our door and Da went wild. Ma was proud of it and let everyone know we were keepin' the country. Ma really didn't have to tell anyone as all the oul' wans'd be watchin' to see where the postman called on D-day. Did some neighbour come up in the world? Won't be long till that lot's gettin' notions of grandeur!

Anyway on the Drive there were three tax payers: a Guinness employee, an ESB employee, and a civil servant. If the situation was desperate a politician would be roped in. The nature of the complaint would be 'bad attitude' or 'not suited to the parish'. His vast experience in traffic control would be better put to use on the Aran islands directing sheep.

These goings on let us all see that really 'the Force' and the rest of us were the same. In fact it would be hard to get summonsed unless you were in a different district. Even then so-and-so knew so-and-so, so that put paid to that. To describe an outlaw:

someone who had used a knife. Sure, the only place he'd be safe afterwards was in the station. Most of the crimes were solved by the clergy sending the culprits down to face up to it. 'Put up no defence, make restitution, throw yourself at the mercy of the court, and do your time.'

Towards the sixties this started to fade as the TV showed a different image of the criminal. Dressed to kill, with fancy cars and plenty of oul' shillings. Sure they were living like the blind oul' fellah in the Phoenix Park. All he sold out was six whole counties. Could you believe it? Instead of a white mansion at the end of his days, he should have been given a white stick in his early ones.

Horse Country

The finest of horses came up and down the Drive. Laundry horses, Jacob's horses and finally the Guinness horses. You could see the pride in their horses that these drivers had, and they knew the route better than the drivers anyway. The driver sitting up there covered in sackcloth and oilskins and the steam coming up from the beasts. Powerful creatures and if you stopped a driver to ask him about his drays you'd want half a day to spare to listen, such was his pride. There and then he'd take out the nose bags and fill them with oats and give you the history of each animal and he might even allow you to put the nose bag on. There was a love there between man and beast I have seldom witnessed since.

The movement of horses up and down served another purpose as there was no peat moss in those times. The best fertiliser came from the dung or horse droppings. If the horses' bowels gave way outside your house it was a little windfall, gathered up in a bucket and carefully dug in around the prized flowers in the garden.

This was another form of currency as there were a few keen gardeners on the road who would always give a few pence for the find, and be glad to get it. The same as everything else no sooner did the value of the dung become public then it led to many a row.

The worst of the horses that plodded their weary way around Crumlin was the coal and log man's nag. Sweet Jasus, the poor oul' horse would always be at death's door. The wheels of the cart were as old as the hills and made of timber encased with steel hoops. To get the best out of the horse the whip was frequently used and it wasn't uncommon to see the poor nag with blood on her mane. We all pitied the horse. But there was little we could do to help her. The answer was arrived at by my oul' fellah. He decided to order logs each week and pass comment on the beast at every opportunity. Now as the log man wasn't stupid he wised up to the fact that it just might be in his own interest to keep the animal in good shape. Once we started to get logs from him a few more neighbours did the same. Now believe it or not if my oul' fellah had run him off the road, so to speak, that would have closed him down to all his clients on our road. You see, that was the way of dealings then, like say some neighbour didn't go along with the Da, things could start to go bump for him in broad daylight as well as in the night.

The Da's plan worked and the horse started to improve. You could see it plain enough and my oul' fellah took to walking around to her field in the evenings to give her an apple or a lump of sugar that maybe had porridge spilt onto it that morning. I could see a kind side to the Da as he'd talk softly to the beast as though he'd known her all his life. In no time at all no sooner would the Da go into the field than Whitey would come at a gallop straight over to him and nuzzle her head against the Da's chest. This went on for years. It let me see that to get the result you want, check the options, and try to find one that's good for goose and gander alike.

The other horse, if you could call him that, was the pig man's. The pig man kept his pigs at the back of his house down towards the 'Naller' or Grand Canal. Now he was more up-to-date, with car wheels on his cart. His job was to collect any waste that could feed the pigs. Sure you could smell him before you saw him. Poor oul' Noelie, the pig man's son, wasn't the full tanner, let alone shilling. Sometimes he thought he had a stagecoach. But fair dues to his oul' lad, Noelie wasn't given a whip, just a bamboo stick with a bit of string on it. To see him standing up there shouting at the horse with the string flying about was something else. The only thing that he was worrying was the swarm of flies. In the end Noelie just gave in and led the horse around Crumlin by hand. Talk about the blind leading the blind.

Some of the bright boys from Flood's pub gave Noelie a taste of porter and that put paid to him. I remember it well. He went from being gentle and simple to plain mad. God help him, the poor divil didn't know who or where or what he was. Needless to say, he was blamed for every wrongdoing in the parish. Shortly afterwards he disappeared. I cursed whoever had spoiled him, and then remembered my granny's saying, 'God pays his debts without money in this world, son. The books are balanced one way or another before you leave it.' My only wish then was that I'd see this balancing.

Wherever you are, Noelie, I hope you have peace and the best of everything as Crumlin was more full of wonder than you could understand.

THE HERO COMES HOME

Winters were something else on the Naller. When it froze over, we all thought we were Hans Christian Andersen without the skates. This was real entertainment and always ended in someone going through the ice. In summer a ready supply of minnow and the odd eel or roach could be caught. Again these prizes could be swopped with the kids who weren't allowed down the Naller 'cause they couldn't swim.

During the summer, Dolphin's Barn Bridge was the handiest spot for us to have a dip and spend the thrupence or fourpence we were given on sweets instead of going either to Tara Street or Iveagh Baths. My mother always knew by the smell of us where we went but she never kicked up about it.

As luck would have it one day a young fellah got caught in a submerged bike as the brother was walking over the bridge, dressed to kill in his Confirmation suit. Naturally, off the bridge he went and got the kid out along with the bike. The police brought him home covered in green slime and a grey blanket to my Ma who smiled and thanked them. Mind you, the coppers kept the bike. As soon as she closed the front door she bet him good-looking for destroying his Confirmation outfit.

We all thought that that was that, but the Lord Mayor, Ben

Briscoe, got wind of it and the brother had to go down to get a medal for bravery along with a certificate and photograph with the Lord Mayor in the Mansion House. This meant another new suit and the way Ma went on about it you'd think the brother would have been better off if he had drowned.

The big night came and the boul' Gussie gets his recognition – photo in the paper and he's a hero to one and all. Next day he goes down to the Naller and throws the medal in the same spot where he pulled the kid out.

'Too much grief,' he says, 'next time I walk.' Now, if you look at it from his point of view, doesn't that make sense?

Part and parcel of maintaining the canal was the dredgers digging deep to keep the canal open for the barges. The trick here was to stay close to the dredger as the 'crayon' operator would shout to his helpers whenever they got a find. There were always forty or fifty bikes taken out. These were looked on as fair game. Move in fast and grab one and off with it in a flash. The Force didn't take any notice as their kids were at the same thing. Even if a bike was damaged it could be scavenged and many a bike was put together from scraps.

To get a head start on puttin' our hands on a find we had to use our wits. This had to be planned. In the first place, we'd go a quarter of a mile or so ahead of the dredger and spot what we and everybody else wanted. Then one or two of my mates would move fifty yards further down, away from the find, and as soon as the bike was landed by the dredger they'd start shouting, 'There's a body over there!'

The consternation would give us all the time we needed. To keep up the commotion, a few bricks would be thrown in by the mates while they jumped up and down in hysteria. Needless to say, one and all – except me – moved with due respect and caution to the spot. As soon as the mates spotted me away with the prize they scarpered and left the onlookers looking on. Jasus, it was gas! They'd be imagining hands, arms and legs for an hour or so until they realised that they'd been had. Can you picture it? Them talking about clergy and guards being notified, and who should do what, and us a mile away with the spoils.

All the fun invariably was at someone's expense. The key was to make sure it wasn't yours. Have a reputation by all means, but back it up, know the order of things, and fit in. Sure we were all like hens really, but we knew every inch of the coop.

Let's take a look at the dump though. It was where the sports stadium now stands. Not a year went by without some kid drowning there, and still it kept us going there to make rafts like a magnet. Making a raft was the best part of it. It was easy enough to make the platform, but in the fifties there were no plastic drums. No, the best we could do would be tin cans or, if we got real lucky, two empty barrels. Now the best of timber went into those barrels. Sure weren't they made by the coopers down in Guinness's? By the time we'd be finished with them they'd be no use to Guinness's. However, there were plenty more where they came from was our attitude.

Back to the raft. Upon completion, the big launch and then somebody always fell in. When he'd go home it wouldn't take long for his ma to arrive round at one house to pass on the info, and that put paid to that.

THE LIBERTIES

Rialto to Patrick Street – well, most of the locals in Crumlin had come out of the inner city so this was our heritage. The Tivo in Francis Street on a Saturday afternoon. The smell of DDT from the seats. If you couldn't walk in you'd be walkin' coming out. All that scratching afterwards, sure you'd be in bits, spots all over, not knowing which was the worst, the cause or the cure.

It's all changed now – high society goes there, not the St Vincent de Paul Society. I paid twelve pound in to see Anita Reeves on stage, all on her own, doing a show, *Shirley Valentine*. She was no Shirley Temple but she was brilliant. One seat for twelve pound, sure, Jasus, when we were goin' there, they wouldn't take that in a week for the whole flea-pit.

Then we'd be off down Francis Street to see the goings on, around to Ash Street to pay our respects to our relatives, or up to St Patrick's Park to pick flowers and run like Herb Elliot until you made it to the Naller at either Dolphin's Barn or Harold's Cross Bridge. Sure the old groundsmen or gotchies hadn't a chance.

I often stood in Clanbrassil Street with Ma waiting on the 81 bus after the Saturday shop and looked across at the advertisement on the wall depicting shoes of the thirties and forties that said simply, in letters two feet high, 'We won't last if our shoes don't.' Neither did. I often wondered did their shoes last *too* long. I asked Ma and she said, 'There's a history there and maybe sometime I'll tell you.' In other words, either she didn't know or what she knew she would never tell me.

The Liberties were great when you think of it. Liberties, me bollocks! The closest they came to a revolt was a rhyme about the Tans:

> *First you're in the khaki*
> *Then you're in the blue*
> *But now you're in the cages*
> *Like the monkeys in the Zoo.*

How in the name o' Jasus could they revolt at any time when the majority of them were either in service, skivvying or drawing British Army pensions? Declaring allegiance to the Republic while earning the King's shilllin'. Sure the poor eejits were so confused they wouldn't know the difference between Oliver Cromwell and Oliver Goldsmith and would probably vote for both if they went up for the Dáil.

The only ones who might have come up with the solution would be either Bang Bang or Johnny Forty Coats and who would listen to them? Maybe that's what had them as they were. How in the name o' Christ did Bang Bang survive all the same? Sneaking up behind you and then in flash, stampin' the ground and at the top of his voice shoutin', 'Bang! Bang!' Many's the fright he gave me, the bugger. He always seemed to come out of nowhere. Once you passed over the Naller at the Barn, from there on to Patrick Street, even over to Stephen's Green, you'd want to be ready for Banger.

Now Johnny Forty Coats was a different kettle o' fish. He kept to himself and made a point of going into as many restaurants as would serve him and out he'd take a wad o'notes that'd choke a culchie. Feet up on the chair opposite him and the odd spit on the floor until they'd get fed up with him. He was safe in our town though and in a way he represented a secret part in all of us. A devil-may-care attitude which stated, 'Take me or leave me – I don't give a fiddler's.'

What about the boul' Mickser Reed strutting around St Teresa's Gardens like the Lord Mayor? All two foot nine inches of him with his shirt open to the waist and his sleeves up. Just for laughs he'd do the odd cartwheel or handstand across from the now closed Johnston, Mooney & O'Brien store. We all knew when Mickser got a part in either a film or play, he told everybody. Sure they'd need no advertising. A right narky bugger though, when the humour was on him. To get even, we used to shout over, 'What are you going to be when you grow up – a bleeding jockey?' The older lads said he was a right bleeding jockey as he was, and this made no sense to us. Can you see the boul' Mickser sitting up there on Silver, 'High Ho, Silver away!' and Tonto looking on in bewilderment? Jasus, you'd have to hold Mickser onto a bar stool. Still, you never knew.

The cinemas started to feel the pinch of the TV. Do you remember Billy Panama, the yo-yo king? Ten yo-yos going up and down and him in his dapper red suit starting up the craze. How about Davy Crockett, the King of the Wild Frontier, or how about 'Rock Around the Clock' in the Star cinema, with the reports of dancing in the aisles, seats ripped up and numerous brawls outside afterwards?

My uncle Peter lived down the back of the pipes on the way to Guinness's before he was married. Peter's sister Joan was a dwarf. Joan, however was built proportionally. Three foot high and looks that would put Hollywood's best to shame. She'd get the part of the good fairy in the Panto. Jasus, we all loved Joan. My suspicions were that the Union, St James's Hospital now, got her with the consumpt. The dread of every Dub was to end up in the Union and no matter how many name changes it gets, to a Dub it stays the Union. Istanbul was once Constantinople, same place. Sellafield was once Windscale, same cancer. Once again some redneck decided to invoke the blessings of the Church and poor oul' St James got the can. Sure if he was alive he'd sue for damages for misrepresentation or misuse of his good name!

BOTTLE

Further across from the Union over the South Circular, was the Stadium. This was the home of boxing. Lugs Brannigan doing ref. Now when it came down to it there were a few different types of boxer as well as weights. The first was the sissy or fellah who everyone gave a dig to, just to watch him run home. His oul' wan would get him into the ring to learn how to defend himself. The only problem about this was that outside the ring there were no refs and the poor gobdaw would only be set up for more of the same. The second type had either a hair lip or stuttered. These seemed to do better as the fire in their bellies would be let out and they'd come on strong inside or outside the ring. The third type was the boxing family. If the oul' fellah here was any use in his day, he'd push his kids whether they had it or not. This just left the kids with a chip on their shoulders and the best scraps they'd ever have would be outside any ring and they'd normally end up in a police station.

The fourth type and the best of the lot would be the natural who only had to be told the rules. Sure you'd pick him out before any bell went and he didn't need any ref for protection, but Jasus help anything that would be facing his fast hands and bottle anywhere. He'd be the fellah we all went to see and sure one round of a bloke like that made your sixpence well spent. One round would be all you'd get as he'd rip any of the first three types apart. This led to problems as no sooner would he be seen to be a rough diamond than he had to be faced.

As leader of my gang it'd be my business to take him on. Otherwise my crew could easily do turncoat and follow the natural. A go-between'd arrange a scrap in the lane on the way out of the Stadium. From my point of view it was a no lose game. None of the gang'd want either the punches I'd throw or collect in the scrap. So one way or the other the order stayed the same. But I made a few right clangers here.

You see, age didn't come into it and I found myself on the deck a few times before I learned that lesson. However, once you had the moxie, that's what counted, to stand up having been put away and simply say, 'I'm not up to you, pal. You're better, fair dues.' And that was the end of that. Normally whoever burst you would tell you where you were going wrong and show you how to counter. This was his duty in those days.

After a year or two the natural would jack up and we'd all miss him. He'd a been a real fighter and by the time he'd get to jack in we'd all be shoutin' for him. You'd be able to smell his bottle and feel the vibration of anger coming from him while he was waiting on the bell. He might not have had much skill but no matter what he'd be hit with, he'd keep coming forward. Nothin' worse than that in a scrap in the ring or outside it. Sweet Jesus, when he'd open up with a combination it'd be all over and Lugs the ref'd have to step in to stop him commitin' murder. With the cost of travel so high and there bein' no money about he wouldn't have a chance of ever makin' a few pound other than side bets as he'd never get to the money boxes in America. The oul' timers around the ring'd say, 'It's a pity we can't bottle his piss and give it to the other wasters we have scrappin'.'

Names or titles would mean nothing to him, only to the dandy boxers. He'd know he was No.1 and so did the rest of us. The best boxers I ever saw in the South Circular Road left with sweet eff-all – except the bone taken out of their noses.

A Star Is Born

Now, we've seen the book and the film *My Left Foot* and we admire the man. Let's go back to poor oul' Christy Brown being pushed in a go-car or summer pram to let the air at him. His lower jaw jutting out, wild eyed, floundering around the pram. One of his brothers pushing the pram and trying to keep the kids away. Jasus, you have to hand it to that family, they kept him out of the circus.

My memory of Christy is of his eyes. They said something or had something to say. Thanks be to Christ he got it said, but did it make up for the deal he got? Only God knows! What did it feel like for him, trapped in a go-car at the whim of whoever took an interest in him? A curio, so to speak, and years later to see him on TV. Sweet Jesus, wasn't that something else? The best of luck to him and a happy release it must have been. Sure he used to remind me of me granny's saying, 'When you're down, down with you.'

I remember the then infamous Brendan Behan puking over Byrnes' wall, at the corner of Sundrive and Clogher roads, into the hedge. The Brylcream or brilliantine running down his face as he suffered the onslaught of a 'woegious' hangover on a Saturday night. In spite of his obvious pain, he had the ability to look down from the gutter at us and see it and us for what we were.

I don't ever remember seeing any of the so-called literary critics – who after his death claimed him a genius – stand beside him when his gut retched yellow bile to match the yellow hedge at that corner. Not many, if any, could claim this. He was like a toy doll to them all. They'd use him for live entertainment in the boozer and laid great claims to their association with him in the hopes that maybe some of his thunder would fall on them.

Well, it did too, as could be seen on TV when we got our own channel. Did you ever hear how some dedicated, loyal would-be-nothin' would change his accent on TV as soon as Brendan's name was mentioned or one of his family appeared? Sure didn't the well-known publican's son lay claim to barring him from his oul' lad's boozer, in Blanchardstown? If you could go back now, Father Clery, you'd hold him in your arms and remember the prodigal son. As a matter o' fact, you're together now, lads. Lord rest both of you.

Another character was the boul' Philo who made it big in the music business. The only bloke in Crumlin who never got a black eye, 'cause he was as black as the ace of spades. Dear Phil Lynott was the only one who didn't know how good he really was. Started his career as lead singer in the Black Eagles, changed over to Skid Row and ended up as Thin Lizzy. Life got complicated for him fast, goin' from a quiet decent bloke to megastar, and megastar he was in more ways than one. He always said he'd go at forty and you don't get much closer.

Makes me kinda nervous, Philo, as we had that one conversation about dying. I'll never forget it. Both of us looking back at Crumlin somewhere about June 1973, and both of us coming down hard, sure it was like we were dead men already. As you saw it the booze had me fucked and as I saw it the drugs had you fucked. Then how in the name of Jasus did you know I'd make it? Two emotional fuck-ups but you gave me hope, and I knew you weren't too smart, so maybe you were telling the truth or saw something I didn't. Sweet Jasus, forty was a long shot for either of us and I'm writing this, Phil, fourteen years sober.

We never met again face to face but as I went further into hell I knew you were doin' fine. I'd often think of you walking down from the chipper in that slow gait. Sure you did fine, Philo, you could do no different. 'Wise up,' people would say, but they didn't know that: 'Some are wise and others are otherwise'. It seems to me that we got the choice of: 'A day like a lion or a life like a lamb'. In another one hundred years who's gonna give a fuck anyway. Sure it'll mean bugger-all to the culchie bird that you told was standing at the wrong Pillar and left you freezing up there in the Phoenix Park. How in the name o' Jasus did she expect a second chance to make a fool of you? You had a way about you, Philo. We needed you and your larks.

THE PILLAR

Nelson Pillar was where all the buses went and if you wanted to meet someone, there was no better spot. We didn't give a fiddler's who was up there, although we heard a few discussions about putting St Patrick or the Pope on top instead. To pay the penny ha'penny and walk all the way up was something else, to see the city scurryin' around below. Just to be there and look down on our town scratching its way to self determination. 'Quo fucking *vadis*,' me oul' fellah'd say. It was said that some bloke threw himself off the top and that's why the cage was fitted. Would you believe it, my bladder always filled up when I went up? Naturally I pissed on the city through the cage. It was also said that one day an umbrella went up when I pissed off the top. Blown up since, the Pillar, and now the buses go to An Lár or the Skivvy. Not really the same thing, is it?

Some genius decided to close down the Harcourt Street train line. I can remember well the steam engines, the excitement, out for the day to the sea. The 22 bus down at Loreto Convent on the Drive, down to Kelly's Corner, see the huge bottles of perfume in the window of the chemist's there, then off over to the station. We were free, bursting at the seams. Where would we sit? Could we manage to get between two carriages so we could stick our heads out the window to get our faces black with soot from the engine? When we'd get to Seapoint, we'd put ha'penny's on the line and let the trains go over them and squash them out to the size of a penny. Many's the slot machine I buggered with them.

But in the end the line was too good for the Dubs, so it had to go. I wonder will we ever find out who did this con job for Mother Éire. A bit like the Pillar. One removal was legal and one was not, but which was which, and what was what?

Gangs visitin' other gangs was part and parcel of our ways. Set up a football match or else rob an orchard together. It wasn't always a punch-up. When all came to all it was the best way of bein' trouble-free. Each of the crews had their own boss, joker and runner and that's the way it stayed. That way we all got along and if you were out on a limb somewhere you could count on a safe haven. Nicknames were direct – Gammy for the bloke with cross eyes or Gimpy for the bloke with the short leg, Skinny and Fatso speak for themselves. No insult given and none taken. On summer days there was always action anywhere.

The scrap heaps just around the corner from the Tara Street Baths were always a good bet. Rumour had it that the scrap metal was for export to Japan to be recycled. Made no odds to us though, if there was a set of wheels there for a gig they were our property and that was that. The trouble here was always the watchman. First you had to spot the wheels. The next part was hard work. Jasus knows what you'd have to move to get them. We'd have to keep the watchman busy while we'd get dug in. This is where team effort came in and tactics were the key. As there were normally three or four heaps, we had to keep the gotchie busy minding the ones without the wheels in them. This normally meant that one of the mates or myself got nabbed but the oul' divils wouldn't know what to do with us. They'd point out that we could be killed if the heaps turned over, threaten us with the police and then have a chat. Sure who wanted to be a stool-pigeon, God gave Ireland more than her fair share of informers already.

While this was going on the wheels would be pinched, but that was only half the job. The worst was yet to come. No sooner would we be seen with them, than every gouger would try to take them from us.

It's a long walk from Tara Street to Crumlin but we knew where to expect the ambushes. Normally the crew from Townsend Street who hadn't even noticed the prize would make first claim. This was fairly even-Stephen as the same iron bars that they could pick up would be available to us. The best means of defence is always attack so we'd have a go on the spot with the nearest bloke and cleave him. This'd astonish his mates and whether they were better than him or not in a row, you can be sure they got discouraged awful fast and backed away to await the next opportunity. From being hard men they'd be talking flatfoot or copper in no time. Once you heard that, you'd won.

Jibe and laugh and one more good run straight at the mouthpiece, and watch the miracle of the disappearin' hard shaws. Mind you, you'd want your wits about you in case either their big brothers or oul' fellahs showed. Remember every face and get the names if possible 'cause in no time you'd meet them again. Normally that was no bother as they wanted in with you from what they'd seen.

Many's the mate and good mate, I met this way. We'd exchange strokes and hang out together. One of these blokes met me eighteen years later in the boozer, and could you believe it, when I was under pressure stood shoulder to shoulder with me? We both walked away! Jasus, by the time he was finished, 'cause he may as well have been on his own for all the use I was, the mouth-pieces with their silent knives were talking flatfoot. Strange, but that day I expected lights out as this time I had nothing to give. I can't mention your name, pal, but you are some dude.

Around by Trinity, off up Grafton Street to Harcourt Street, up to the Naller and then the only Indians we'd meet would be more than likely to know us, with the one exception, Portobello where the Hollyfield crowd hung out. The same rules applied here so we'd split up and hide the prize. One lot of us would taunt them into a claim down at Mount Pleasant and the runner would make for home with the wheels. As soon as the Hollyfield crowd bit, run like Billio down by the grocery shop, through the arch and into Mount Pleasant Square. It was all down to speed. We knew which of the railings in the Square were broken and allowed one at a time through. This was a real treat, in behind the railings and waiting. Now the trick was to pull the opposition through by any means, clothes or arm or leg or hair, the railings did the rest. Needless to say, the Hollyfield gang copped on and it became a vendetta.

That was the first time I remember a knife being pulled on me. I must have been nine or so. Times were changing! The gouger was more surprised to see the knife open in his hand than anyone else, however, it was in his hand. This caused consternation in the ranks and my mates and me froze. It was like the field with young O'Brien again with no back-up. I can still see him looking down at his knife admiring it. That was the last thing he saw that day other than a doctor, as he got the best of a rusty railing on his collarbone. You'd want to hear the screams and then he passed out. We vanished through to Leinster Road and down Larkfield to home and safety as that was a Maria job, juvenile or not.

Patience is a great thing and needless to say his brother got me that summer. One on one as agreed through go-betweens. The stage was set and I got battered. Afterwards, he explained to me their set-up and who the family were. Would you believe it, one of me own bleedin' relations? Jasus, if we'd all stayed in Ash Street with me Da's relatives, we'd at least see one another now and again. We realised that this was now a family matter. I told the brother Gussie the story and off he goes as the same age difference applies. The only problem is that the brother is classified by some quack as 'dangerously violent' so Jasus only knows what's coming.

At this stage my oul' fellah found out that something was going on, and I gave. Off with him like a shot and me in the back of the car. We catch up with the brother at Harold's Cross Bridge, and me oul' fellah can't get him to stop. Eventually we get him into the car and he tells the oul' fellah there's always tomorrow or the day after – and he's not joking.

I wished to Jasus I was dead! Who in hell wanted all this grief? But my oul' man wasn't stupid and simply said he'd deal with it and call there and then. Both my brother and myself found out that night all about bottle. No fuss, just called up a few memories, and promised to build up oul' Tommy and his sons with cod liver oil before he'd slap them. This kinda settled things and the brother and myself shut up as it was obvious that the oul' fellah didn't hold our relations in high esteem in any department. The hatchet was buried and that was that. When we got home me mother was up the walls and the oul' man just said, 'Enough is enough and no more talk about it.' And there wasn't. This was one of the few times I ever saw my oul' man stand out and believe you me it was no joke. The oul' fellah was built like a tank and fit as a fiddle, sure you'd have to be nuts to cross him with his dander up.

The clock ticks on and in our time both me brothers and myself gave the oul' man a doin's in the sixties and early seventies. Lord be good to him, he could take it and give it but the clock was against him. I was the youngest and last to do him. He was as proud as punch with all of us. He died in 1972 shortly after my scrap with him, and we hadn't spoken since that day. His oul' heart gave out but he came conscious for a minute on his way out and winked at me. That was enough for both of us as we weren't real talkers anyway.

My oul' man always maintained that there were two types of people. Those with backbone and those with wishbone for backbone, and the wishbone merchants mouthed. Any time I think of him I do as he said and remember the good times. He'd had a hard life and he expected the world to do the same to us. His fear for our safety and security made him as tough as nails on us. Wouldn't you know, Da, you were dead right!

VISITING THE UNCLES

Me great-uncle Ned chose to end his days in Rathdrum in the old County Home. As we were his nearest and dearest we'd visit him every second month. On the way there we'd often see either the Tinkers or Jews travelling to Dublin with duck or down mattresses on the tops of their cars. The Tinkers'd be drivin' the Ford Ten Hundredweight vans and the Jews their cars, and the ticks or feather mattresses, destined to become pillows or be exported to Europe, would be tied to the top.

This was a worthwhile business as with the new Dunlop mattresses the bright boys were able to give a swop. New Dunlop mattress for your old duck or down one, and a few pound on top for your back pocket.

Horse hair was another trade the boys were in and nylon was only beginning to show its face. Slowly but surely the trade dried up, and the population of five and a half thousand Jews started to dwindle.

Da said the Jews had come from Latvia or Estonia at the end of the last century and set up here selling crucifixes and rosary beads from door to door.

As time went by they grew into the money lending. The cost of a one pound note was a shilling for the week – a ten-shilling note lent on a Monday'd cost eleven shillings on that Friday.

Many's the child made his or her First Holy Communion or Confirmation on these borrowed funds. In its own way it supported the dignity of the families. Who else'd give them the loan? They would be too afraid to walk into a bank, let alone ask for a loan. What porter worth his salt would've let them in? The pride in our national religion led to many's the broken family.

Granny and Da'd have a right set to when he'd say he was out with one of his pals, Solly. 'First we're helpin' Jews then we're helpin' Germans, who in the name o' Jasus is helpin' us?' she wanted to know. 'That's right, son, you an' your likes keep helpin' them up onto their horses and mark my words,' she'd go on.

The Da'd just turn the other cheek, but when Granny had gone home he'd tell Ma, 'If I ever see that woman in this house again that's the end of her.' Needless to say, the Ma took no notice and nothin' ever happened over the few words.

Sad to see the Jews going, there's only a thousand or so left in the country. Well-established in the professions. How many are left in our little Jerusalem? The call of Israel seems to be their call of the wild. 'Next year in Jerusalem.'

The same thing is happenin' to the Tinkers the only difference is they're sayin', 'Next year in the council house or serviced site.'

Anyway, me great-uncle Ned gave me two ten-shilling notes to buy a good .22 rifle on his deathbed at ninety-seven years of age. He'd been hiding his life's savings under the oilsheet on his bed for years. All in all, twenty pounds or forty ten-shilling notes. To see him hand over his fortune to us and decide on his funeral! Jasus, he thought you'd be able to buy a farm for the twenty pounds. Sure, the grave alone cost a tenner. I couldn't tell him that you'd hardly get a pellet gun for one pound.

The stately way Ned told the nuns in the home to clear off, bad an' all as he was, while he put his affairs in order, was real class. Crippled with arthritis, his fingers buckled, riddled with rheumatism and pneumonia in his lungs, but a man full of love. That was my great-uncle Ned. His eyes stayed young and so did his heart. He'd tell me to ignore the so-and-so nuns and go out to the nuns' orchard and take all I wanted. Strange though, I never did as somehow I felt that after we'd go, he'd maybe have a price to pay. A born batchelor, as were his two brothers Mike and Ted. All made it to the ninety years plus on this planet. He'd joke and say, 'Stay a bachelor and raise your children the same way.'

On the way home Da'd let me out to collect wild crab apples in Rathdrum so we could make the jelly, but on that last trip we hadn't the heart. I still see those loving eyes as he held me and said goodbye. As far gone as he was he told me: 'God has only one measure of time and that's a life, men made calendars. Walk out the corridor like the man you are and let them all see courage.'

I made it outside all right, Ned, but went into a rage as at eight years I knew what was going on. I kicked the doors downstairs until me shoes burst and my feet bled, I ripped an apple tree to shreds and then peace came.

My Ma and Da came down and it was all over. Ned had held on to see us and could go on no more. Jasus, how could he love us so much? I wish we could travel back and get the two ounces of Warrior Plug Tobacco and Marietta biscuits for you, Ned, and maybe I will in a lifetime.

Ned's brother, Ted, lived in Skerries. He was a First World War or Great War veteran in the British Army and was all over India and Africa as well. His stories were fact and he'd tell you he was no hero – Clint Eastwood wasn't born yet. So we got a firsthand report on history. Ted would talk matter of fact about wild fancy places and tell of strange goings on.

Anyway, as usual with our lot, something strange was going on. He'd write up and say that the house was being up-ended at night. Naturally we thought it was the gargle and him doing it himself. This was not the case though. Once again me Da was called out to resolve matters.

First the brother was sent down to the house to Ted to check out the story of the so-called hauntings, as the Da put it. The Ma knew full well that me oul' fellah thought there was insanity on her side of the family, he said it often enough. But, Jasus, he was comin' close to gettin' proof. Well, when the brother comes back and confirms the story Da kinda looks at him as much as to say 'you too'.

Ted was after reporting the doin's to the Gardaí who didn't want to know. Then he reported it to the priest who in his own good time came to visit the house.

Well, off to Skerries to sort it out went Ma, Da and us kids. When we walked into the house the chill went up our spines. Ted had gotten himself a big dog and the bowler wouldn't go into the house. Jasus, we all felt it. However, as always, Da took charge and put us out in the yard while he talked with Ted. As it turned out a force was lifting him up and throwing him against the walls, sure he had bruises all over. Next, the dog was dragged in and went mad to get out. My senses told me there was evil there and I wasn't proven wrong.

The Ma was delighted when he told her. Whatever the neighbours had we had one over on them. Then the Da told her it wasn't exactly a prize and Ted wanted rid of it.

Home with us all and back down with Da. He wanted us far

away when the presence showed, and show it did. Between the priest and the bishop, the guards and Da and Ted, the deal was done and an exorcism duly authorised and completed. If it worked somebody forgot to tell the unholy ghost, the Da said.

Ted decided Skerries was too much and his fear of the house never really left him. He decided to go to the Chelsea Pensioners Home in London and we'd see him on telly once a year all decked out in his uniform until he passed away. It used to drive Ted mad that he had fought in all those wars and the Free State government wouldn't let him wear his uniform to commemorate the battles he was in and the dead friends left behind. His medals were left to Ma and, after she died, robbed out of the house. If anyone ever shows you Ted McGuinness's medals he's either a thief or a receiver, wittingly or unwittingly.

The third brother, Mike, was a different story. Mike loved Dublin and thought he owned St Stephen's Green. He'd walk around by the statues showing the thread of life which was presented to the Irish people by the Germans as appreciation for our help after the war. These three statues are at the Leeson Street corner of the Green and the only use I could see for them was to jump over the pond and hold onto them and to jump off to the far side. Mike was full of the Green and never missed a day in it. Hail, rain or snow, Mike strolled the Green and I'd often spot him there. He lived over in Heytesbury Street so it was close enough for the oul' fellah.

Oul' uncle Mike used to break his sides laughing when I'd tell him of my goin's on. He never gave out to me though and if I was under pressure at home for being missing I'd just say, 'Sure I met oul' Mike and I couldn't walk off on him.' Mike was always good for a Player and he used to watch me puff away. I'd gum it and chew half the tobacco and, looking back, I see it was his way of holding on to me for company. I'd tell Mike everything about my antics and he'd give me a few coppers and say he didn't know what I was growin' into.

Neither did I, Mike, but I looked after you when you had the stroke, never left you without a visit when you were down in the Meath Hospital even though I didn't think you knew I was there. Me Da said the only time you were in a Mercedes was when you were in the pine box. I was sad about that as you were a big shot to me, knowing Jimmy O'Dea and Noel Purcell, and them knowing you, more's to the point. The Hibernian's gone now so is St Vincent's Hospital and Cullen's pub. You'd hate to see what they did at the top of Grafton Street. Progress, it's called, Mike.

It's as well you're not strolling around Stephen's Green these days, as you'd probably be mugged, while some gallant member of the Force or Gardaí would run or drive in the other direction if he saw you in trouble. Their answer now is, 'You shouldn't be there,' and sure maybe they're right. After all, if they could only keep everybody at home all the time they'd have it made. Promotions on parking tickets, and then to the Garda Club on their way to get dried out in the park, or St Patrick's. What more could they ask for?

DUBLIN'S GARDEN OF EDEN

To me, the Green meant chestnuts, feeding the ducks, floating the rafts made from lollipop sticks, and flowers for me Ma. In winter, if it was really cold and the duck pond froze over, we'd be on the ice. Sweet Jesus, when you think of it, it was Paradise. The keepers scrambling on the ice to chase us off even when it was solid. When it thawed a bit, we'd check it out, and spot a way of crossing which we guessed would hold us. For the crack, we'd wait around till a keeper spotted us, and when he was a few yards away from us, we'd make a dash across the ice. Naturally his instinct was to follow, however, if our reckoning was right we'd make it and he'd go through clean as a whistle. Jasus, he'd be up to the waist and fuming, then out would come the whistle and he'd blow like fuck. We blew too.

One November, the Green ponds were frozen solid. Some students from Trinity College came up with ice skates. Jasus, they were brilliant! We wouldn't a even known where to rob ice skates, let alone use them. The keepers were wore out trying to get them off. The students zigzagging this way and that and the keepers goin' on their arse at every turn. It was great. A carnival on ice for free with clowns thrown in with whistles – what more could ya want? There was a crowd gathered of about two hundred in no time. It was fairly put up to the keepers so what did they do but all got off the ice. Some smart bollocks of a keeper had spotted the students' shoes and books and that's what he used to blackmail them all off the ice. The students had to give in and the keepers thought they had it made, goin' to take names an' all.

The whole crowd took exception to the bollocks's attitude and in no time they were surrounded and threatened by what was there. 'It's a free country!' was the cry and the keepers were treated like informers. They hadn't a choice if they wanted to stay healthy other than to make a peace with the mob to the mob's satisfaction, and that was simple enough. 'Put your pencils away,' one oul' fellah said, 'and forget the faces or yours'll be well remembered.' I don't know who he was but, Jasus, he wasn't really asking, nor jokin'.

When the keepers put away their pencils and the smart bollocks gave back the books under the stranger's supervision and not a word spoke, he kinda let the keepers take over again with his permission if you like. He just walked off without another word. Pity the keepers didn't do the same, they started up their cry again of 'off the ice'. Them keepers are like fuckin' oul' wans, no wonder we tormented them any chance we got what else could we do?

On hot summer days, to nip into the fountains and splash one and all was the crack. What did the buggers do but empty the fountains just in case people used them. There had to be some bloody redneck brother of some politician running the Green. No football, no walking on the grass, no throwing sticks up to get the chestnuts and no water in the drinking fonts most of the time. Sure you'd need eyes in the back of your head to have a lark.

A gang of us would go up to the old ruins of the manor house in the Green and play Cowboys and Indians and then after the inevitable chase by the keepers, across by the toilets and out on to Grafton Street. Here was a shop to beat all shops: Geary's Toy Store. Just to look in the window and see the model planes and trains was a delight.

Christmas time was the best though. Down Grafton Street to see how the other half lived. The smell of coffee as you'd go past Bewley's, on down to the 'nob' shops. What about the Green Cinema or the Grafton Arcade cinema? Mind you, we couldn't afford them, but they were there. The traffic jams were great too. Just to watch the drivers effing one another out of it and to shout over and egg them on. Some days we'd cut across by the Gaiety Theatre and see what was on there, then off over, up by Dockrell's timberyard and into St Patrick's Park.

It seemed all the oul' war veterans thought they owned it. Strutting around with the campaign medals on their coats for one and all to see. Half of them were probably bought in the pawn, so we didn't put great store in their stories, poor lonely oul' divils. They'd even give you a Woodbine if you'd listen to their war heroics. Sure we knew it all from the comics in the hairdresser's. They'd always have loads of advice to give, harmless sorts, but divil the advice I took.

Off over through the Tenters, up by the knackers, through to Donore, and up Clogher Road, back to home. 'Where were you?' was next. 'Out and about,' was the answer and that was that. Once or twice I had to go to the Meath Hospital with cuts, and then I'd have to give a full account of the day's doin's. The bastardin' hospital smell always gave me away. Other days the route home was up through the Coombe by the old maternity hospital. It looked like a jail! I couldn't understand the oul' wans who said the only time they got a rest was in there. Babies, babies and more Jasus babies was all I saw coming out of it and who in their right minds wanted the screamers? Doesn't life change? On up to the Drive and left to home, shelter under the trees if it was raining, and then make a burst for home.

Dolphin's Barn was hardly worth a stop. Sure the flicks on in either the Leinster Picture House – that's the skating rink now – or the Rialto, now Windsor Motors, would be antiques. The only attraction here was the hardware and the only items we ever wanted were rat traps and slings. Jasus, the fun you could have with a rat trap was something. Mind you, they were delicate and could break your fingers if you weren't careful. We'd get an old handbag and fill it with paper and place the trap underneath, leave it out when no one was looking and get behind a wall and wait for the sucker.

Now we'd have to pick our mark as, if it was a grown up, it was goodbye to our trap. We'd nip in and out four or five times till the right kid came. To see him or her dancing around with the trap snapped on their hand! Get the trap back and they'd be in on the next set-up. The other trick was to get a handbag and put a bit of thread on it. When the mark bent down, just move it a bit. It used to be great gas to see some well-to-do push the bag over with his or her foot to the wall, before going down. They'd check all around first and then go for it and we'd all come out laughing, but some of the gits took it to heart and came after us. Sure they'd no hope as we'd cross the walls over to the field at the back of the Drive like lightning, and leave them with their threats.

EXAMPLE AND ADVICE

'Saturday night fever' had a meaning all of its own for us back in the fifties. Since we'd come through the Emergency, just about, we had the luxury of Sunlight and carbolic soaps. Furthermore, other luxuries were available – syrup of figs and senna-pods.

Lamb o' Jasus but the Saturday night check-up was something else. Ma gathered us round and said 'Strip', and the inspection started. Cuts and boils – for bread and soap poultices to be put on red hot. Jasus, the screams. Next the dose of syrup, one of us after the other. 'Never mind if you have the runs, it'll do you a power of good.' All five of us at the same time. Sure it was like the Grand National. If we hadn't a row over who was lingering in the jacks, one was sure to follow the next operation. Head lice and bath.

The bath was filled to the brim and in went the eldest. First-class shampoo and conditioner – a new Sunlight brick – the two in one. If Ma was holding back the Sunlight for the washing, it was carbolic, and you'd smell a right bolic all week. We all took our turn by age, down to me. Just when I'd be getting out, one of the others would say they'd pissed in the bath and all hell'd break loose.

The oul' fellah, who up to now had been reading the paper at the fire, would be called to sort us out. 'Fucking animals!' he'd roar and start ranting to himself about Ma not being able to control us. Next the big threat: 'If I have to take charge here you won't know what's what!' Out the hall he'd come and up the stairs shouting 'Silence!' Sure he only made things worse because, if he got within hand's reach of you, you got a clatter and started roaring.

With our lot though, over the years, Da's stageshow bit didn't carry much weight. We reckoned he was as much fair game for us, coming up the stairs as we were for him when he got to the top. Shoes, socks and anything else we could throw at him got thrown. Many's the time I saw him nursing his head and glaring at us, 'Which of you threw this or that?' No answer. Then he'd screech with his arms outstretched to the heavens, 'God grant me patience but I have to get to Christ away from this mad house.' Off he'd go, and Ma would start up, 'Now look at the state you have him in. Jasus only knows if he'll ever come back.' But he always did 'cause we were his.

We might not have been much like the Foley family on the radio, with oul' Tom and Alice ever so reasonable and nice to one another, but we had a cast-iron edge on everyone – we were loved. The Da often said to me that he made as many mistakes being a father as I did a son, 'but no worry, it's both our first times.'

September coming and school starting up again. The only good thing then to look forward to was the chestnuts. Now once again, there are a few types of chestnuts and you had better know which was which. In summer, when the chestnut trees flowered, there were two colours – white and pink. Now the white ones were all over the place, Stephen's Green, the Phoenix Park, and every cat, dog and divil from Kenilworth to the sea had one of them. No, the pink one was the one you wanted, ready to be roasted at the fire on the poker and duly eaten.

The oul' fellah took great pride in telling me the difference and I kept it to myself. He told me the difference in the leaf too, but to be on the safe side I used to mark my trees. Now you'll say to yourself, where in the name of Jasus is he going to pull out pink chessers? Simple, down the Naller at the back of Griffith Barracks. Mind you, they were on the wrong side of the wall but not for long. Wouldn't it have been lovely had we known a Commandant or such like who could have walked us straight through to the chessers? Fat lot of luck! All we knew were barely hanging on in there themselves, or else would let on that they didn't know us anyway. No, the only way was the hard route and sure that way – the fact that the chessers were eaters stayed safe. Between climbing and barbed wire and nettles and more nettles, Jasus, you'd say, was it worth it?

Sure the Germans would've had no hope of getting into Griffith Barracks whether Hitler had a said so or not. We'd get to the trees and it would take an hour or so to load up. As luck would have it, there was always some oul' soldier who would report us, and, Jasus, you'd think we were Hitler's lot with their goings on over a few measly chestnuts. Green uniforms shouting at green uniforms and us at the once. 'Fuck them! What do they think they have in there, the crown jewels?' However, once they'd cottoned on to us it was time for high-ho. You see, once we were the Naller side of that fence we could eff and blind at them all we liked and they were banjaxed. But before long some green uniform would start talking blue uniform and then *we'd* be banjaxed.

Back over through the yard at Harold's Cross Bridge, and back down through the Cross to the Drive. This meant we had twenty different ways of arriving home as against going up Clogher, which would have left us wide open to the Force if they'd been called. After the divvy up I used to ask myself if it was worth it. How an' ever, it filled the day for us and kept us out of harm's way – shilling gas meters, tapping telephones – you know yourself.

Years later, where would you believe was I invited but down to the bossman's house in the boul' Griffith Barracks on the South Circular Road to a party, no less. The whole bleeding place opened up to me! If only time could stand still.

Sure now I'm talking Barracks, what about our own shortcut through from Harold's Cross Bridge to Rathmines? Nip down by the side of the cottages, leg up onto the Barracks wall and straight across to Rathmines. The only dodgy bit was coming out of the Barracks if there was something special on. Then the sentry wanted to know how in the name of Jasus we were there at all. Brazen it out. 'The fellah at the far side said it was all right 'cause he knows you.' 'What's his name?' Then panic followed. If there was any major delay factor we'd say, 'Thanks be to Jasus we asked you for nothin'.' This always worked and on with us over to Rathmines. So much for the 'Who goes there?' and 'Advance friend and be recognised.' Guff!

The only real trouble we got into was the day we tried to borrow a .303 from the fellah on the gate. Such a gobshite you wouldn't believe. Us standing outside and admiring his gear, next we'd build him up like, ask him does he know Rommel and so on. Then he tells us how to get into the Army, the money, shows off the uniform to a T. Jasus, he even knows MacArthur. The fool, sure everyone knows MacArthur, he lives in Drimnagh. While all this oul' chat was going on we were getting nearer and nearer to the spoils, left standing there just asking to be took. Well, I had a go and the weight of it did me in. I dropped the Jasus thing! Can you believe it? The gobdaw didn't see the funny side of it and clattered me. How an' ever, it was worth a try as that crowd at the top of the Drive would have got their come-uppance with their bleedin' pellet gun and all.

Now, when all comes to all we needn't have worried a bit about the Larkfield shower as who do they shoot at with their so-and-so pellet gun but a Force's son? That put paid to their artillery and it's probably still in the station. Can you just see it? A forty-shot repeater costing forty-five shillings, as black as coal. When I told me oul' fellah that I wanted one for me birthday, what did I get? A fishing rod. He says, 'If you're that interested in sport, make do with this.'

After the initial shock wore off, I went out on the Drive and started casting this way and that. Up the road with the lead weight, down the road, over the road and over the fuckin' telephone wires it went. Out came the oul' fellah and he couldn't believe it. Anyway, he took the rod and reeled in as much line as he could, and then cut the line. Then he leaned over to me and said: 'Now you've lost your weight and ten yards of line, haven't you?'

What else could I say but 'Yes', but the next part was beautiful. 'Now, son, you've learnt when to cut your losses, and never forget it.' I never did, Da, but it's still the pulling and tugging I do before I cut that gives me the most grief.

THE INEVITABLE

No sooner would something new such as the fishing rod come into the house than it led onto somethin' else. Havin' a fishing rod and what's left of the line along with the oul' fellah's grandest advice, the next thing to do was go fishing. Naturally I'd need bait, the brod says worms or dough'd be no use, as every gobdaw fished with them. The best bait, he reckon, is chandlers, so off to get them.

Straight to the tanner's yard down in Watling Street, milk bottle in hand. I was halfway to catchin' Moby Dick. I'd no bother gettin' all the bait I wanted as the oul' fellahs down there didn't get too many visitors – for obvious reasons. They only had to show me the skins and give me the go-ahead and it only took two or three skins to half-fill the bottle with chandlers. I asked the gaffer would he let me in the odd day as I was startin' up some serious fishing. He agreed and I could see in me mind's eye the queues outside my house payin' a penny for ten chandlers. Jasus, I was goin' to be rich.

Back up Watling Street and what's at the top but a cart with one of the horses down. The look of his front leg said it all, he wasn't comin' back up. The leg askew at the knee and the skin ripped from the crash into the cobblestones. It was like somethin'

you'd see in the butchers. The driver cut loose the other dray-
horse and brought him roughly to the back of the cart and tied
him up there. The poor beast on the ground wasn't goin' anywhere, though he kept on trying to get up. Finally the driver sat
on his neck and kept talkin' to him. The wild frantic movement
slowed but the wide eyes stayed.

By now a crowd had gathered, I felt I'd known the wounded
horse all my life and his eyes wouldn't leave me. Then a guard
and a vet arrived. The horse knew it, the crowd knew it, the vet
knew it and, worst of all, I fucking knew it. So it was done. No
loud bang, just a soft thud as the majestic beast became history.
After the thud he jerked for a few seconds and my heart
pounded, just maybe he'd get up on the third jerk like the good
Lord himself, maybe it'd be different for a horse. I allowed
meself hope as his legs flailed. Even I could see the movements
were jagged. As they stopped my hope died. The tears ran down
my face. I looked around and saw many's the wet eye. What
fucking use were vets anyway? All that learnin', sure any idiot
in uniform could do what he had done – or could they? I knew
I couldn't.

Didn't take long for the guard to take charge. 'Off with you
lot. There's nothin' more for you to see here.'

Slowly we all moved away, heads down, back to what we
were doin' before. I took me time home with me chandlers and
decided not to go fishing for a few days.

'Today's horse is tomorrow's harness and that's that' – me
fucking granny again. Some day I'll stump her. You see, Granny
and me had a love-hate relationship, sure you'd only be payin'
her a compliment if you called her a witch.

Whenever she'd be stuck and say she'd missed the bus, I'd
tell her, 'No bother to you, Granny. Just use the oul' brush in the

kitchen, that'll do ya.' Well, the look she'd give me always made me feel I'd never get one over on her. So one day her and me has a right set too. I tell her I'm not goin' to her funeral when she goes. Jasus, but what does she do but make me swear it. Then says, 'Least I'll rest easy knowin' there's one less of you lot there.' She went farther, 'The young must die as well as the old,' she says. True enough, Granny, but the odds are against you, I says. They were too.

It didn't take long to get over my grief for the horse. Granny saw to that. She wanted to know who got the horse's hair. 'And you standin' there and all you had to do was ask,' she said. How could you talk to that? I told her she'd better watch out after her own bleedin' hair and decided to clear off and wet me fishing line. You just couldn't win.

When she died, a few years later, I stayed home and kept my side of the bargain. Me Ma didn't see it that way and I got a clatterin'. Jasus, Ma didn't lick it up in the street, and Granny was one up on me again. Would I never learn? I'd heard that saying, 'Reachin' out from the grave', but this was ridiculous.

Off over to the Green the next day to let me great-uncle Mike know about the horse, otherwise he'd think I'd forgotten him. Oul' Mike wormed it out of me, the reason I told him everything. Jasus, if he died before I filled him in, neither of me grandads would know how their pride and joy was doing 'cause he wouldn't be able to tell. I told him to make sure he told Granny too. The one that was dead, sure the other one would kill me. Fair dues, Mike, you never told a sinner. I hope you told a few souls though. Still our hearts spoke, no matter what. No jibbers present when we met.

DA'S JOB

Our family was fortunate the Da had a good job and had worked his way up the ladder in Guinness's. This meant that there were always a few pounds to spare. No sooner would Da or Ma have it saved then some relation came a cropper and bang went the nest egg. Still the Da never gave up on any of the clan.

I remember him tellin' the Ma he was gettin' a promotion and going on the clerical staff proper. She told him if he got any more promotion he could wash his own shirts and starch the collars as she'd had enough. But I knew she was only keepin' him in check, she was so proud of him even when he got things all mixed up.

Ma used to worry about his health and the Da'd go mad when she'd tell him his age. Just to prove a point he swam his last race at fifty-six years of age and won it. Our house was full of his cups from swimmin'. He used to give them away to his mates and get the inscription of his name rubbed out so they could have somethin' for their sideboards. As he said, 'I did it, son. I know the feelin'.' He left me four cups he wouldn't let go of and a wooden crucifix he won for Catechism at school at six years of age. The wood still carries the mark of his teeth from biting on it when he had a toothache – and of mine for the same reason.

That last race was one too many, but even though he only lived a further two years maybe it was worth it. The pride in his face as he handed the medal to Ma, it seemed as though forty years dropped away and she was his queen for that moment. Jasus, they could go through hell and high water together. But both him and her knew it was his last even though neither said so.

His eyes were red from the chlorine in the water but that didn't cause the tears down his cheeks. The Ma took the medal and put it on the mirror over the fireplace and told him she wanted to be able to see both sides of it at once, but she wished to God he'd grow up. He laughed and told her he had no intention of growing up if it meant bein' feeble.

I loved the days I went down to Da's job to visit him over at the Jetty. It was even better if he wasn't there. He was some sort of boss and the drivers of the mini-gauge railway trains would let me up to drive when he was missing. Da's job would break your heart, controlling the uncontrollable and then coming home to our gang. Sweet Jesus, no wonder he went at fifty-eight. Sure the man upstairs in the great wherever saw he'd had enough. I can just see him checking the loads on to the barges going down to the big Guinness ships or to the B&I, seeing who was sober enough to load and drive. Trying to keep them sober long enough to get the job done. When he went missing it just meant that he was gone back over to the Tap to get the crew out. This was one of the official drinking places in the brewery.

In one gate, out the other, mini-gauge train, the crew, and my oul' man. His problem was being the boss. All the crew were his mates. He was either at school in Franner – the Francis Street school – with them, or else swam with them in the Iveagh Baths. I think he thought he was a social worker really because whenever there was grief he was the man. Always on the side of the underdog, no matter what. Sometimes, he'd take me into his confidence and spell out what was going on.

His best aid to helpin' any crewman was the Guinness rulebook. He knew it by heart and could always find two counterbalancing rules to stagnate any disciplinary action. If the poor bugger who was in trouble didn't spot it, the Da would have to tell him through an intermediary. There'd be my oul' fellah giving out hell, threatening this and that at the top of his lungs to some poor divil the worse for drink. If the poor bugger took it to heart, the oul' man would point out later that the procedure Da had followed was incorrect and therefore invalid as per the rulebook, Section C, Paragraph 2b, Rule 126, and accordingly no disciplinary action was required. He told me it was only a game, just to get the job done and make sure no one got hurt. 'Sure we're all only passing through,' he'd say.

When it came down to it, the only real power was the script. Now the script was a docket the oul' fellah would issue to anyone who was doing fine. It entitled the holder to anything from two pints to twenty-two pints in the Tap. Nothing narked me Da more than some other boss interfering with his operation. Jasus, you'd hear the rulebook then. 'It's bad enough that I know what's going on without that fucking so-and-so know-all passin' comment,' he'd say. Say one word about his crew and, Jasus, the oul' fellah went into print. Reason for no activity: the elements – tide; wind; rain; ice; danger to human life. Backed up by rule such-and-such. Next, the supply insufficient to keep his team on the go. 'Could your Right Honourable Self-Appointed Expert talk to Lord Iveagh about it? ' the Da'd say to the know-all. 'You'll have my blessing. Mind you, you might be stepping on a few toes if you do. Are you planning on leaving the brewery, boyo?'

The Jetty's gone, so is the mini-gauge rail, and the big-hearted men who worked it. All just passed through. You were dead right, Da. Horses, barges and men too, all went down the river in the name of progress. I wonder was the fellah who did this any relation to the fellah who closed down Harcourt Street railway line?

The Balance of Nature

Now between cats and dogs in the house you'd think we had enough going on, but next thing the brother, Dangerously Violent, buys me a pet rabbit. Sweet Jesus, next he'd be turning the other cheek instead of 'in with the loaf first'.

Never mind, I grabbed the rabbit and christened him Bugsy. Now the oul' fellah kicks up, not about the rabbit but about the name. He said we should have called it anything else 'cause the name Bugsy might be taken up wrong – the neighbours might think the rabbit had lice.

For the sake of peace I agreed with him and didn't say a word about him being too late as I'd already done the bit with the holy water. After a while he forgot anyway and things were dandy. Then Bugsy ate up every plant in the garden and him and the cat were always after one another. 'Jasus, can they not get on together?'

One Saturday, Bugsy escaped out the front when Paddy the paperman was coming up the road. Paddy's dog Spot did Bugsy in. I wasn't there and the brother brought what was left of him home. All I could see was my beautiful pal torn open and his tiny heart thumping. I held him till his heart stopped because I knew he would sense some safety from me. Then I laid my little pal down on his favourite spot in the back, and off out to sort out the dog.

There was the boul' Paddy and who do you think was talking to him but my oul'man? They tried to tell me that this was the law of nature and that was that. Then Paddy offered to buy me a new rabbit. I told him to buy a new dog because he was going to need one. I grabbed Spot and he didn't even try to bite me, more's to my surprise. 'Where's this law of nature?' I punched him and he started to whimper. Then Paddy started to cry and my oul' fellah grabbed the dog off me and clattered me! I had another run at the dog and all hell broke loose. The dog ran off out of my oul' man's arms and away like a flash. Next I knew, my own oul' fellah stuck a dig on me straight in the chest. I was winded and out of the game. Sitting there on the ground on my arse, and that bastardin' dog getting off.

Jasus, when I looked at my Da I couldn't believe it. 'Fucking turncoat! Your time will come too. When God made it, he made plenty of it. It's lights out for Bugsy but his pal plans on staying around a while.' I voiced my feelings on the subject to all present which resulted in the oul' fellah grabbing me and dragging me home. Jasus, the commotion. I told Paddy not to bother with a collar for his mongrel anymore, I had one and he'd only need it for a minute, a snare. As we got nearer home I kind of got quiet and the oul' lad felt it too. He didn't go on anymore abut the row but started talking to me about what we should bury Bugsy in. He gave me an old shirt and I scooped my little pal up and dug the hole, me heart broken. I laid him to rest in his spot and wondered what I'd done in life that was so bad to deserve this.

A few weeks went by and I noticed Paddy didn't bring the dog anymore. Ah, some day he'll appear, I says to myself. Another month and, Jasus, I had to ask.

Paddy started apologising and buying more rabbits. Finally I got some sense out of him. He had kept the dog home, locked in the back, because he knew I'd get it on the Drive.

I said nothing but thought to meself, Jasus, Paddy loves his dog and my way isn't really the answer.The next time I met Paddy we called a peace. I couldn't bring Bugsy back. Maybe there was something to this law of nature. It's easy enough to kill but only God creates.

I asked the oul' fellah and he went on and on about a balance and what happened when man interfered with it an' all. I was sorry I opened my mouth. For a second opinion I asked the Absolute Authority who said the oul' fellah was right, but said I was always to remember the first part which was simple: Survive first at whatever the cost. Then and only then, worry about what the oul' fellah was saying about the balancing bit.

More Balancing Acts

Another balancing bit was when we went to rob apples. Let me tell you our best way of getting the supply. While on your travels around the city, summer or winter, keep an eye out for glass-topped walls. You can be pretty sure that the trees in the garden behind the walls are either apple or pear. You could get real lucky and maybe they'd be Granny Smiths.

The bits of broken glass were a dead giveaway, a bit like a marker buoy at sea, except to our mob it meant that on the far side was the Garden of Eden. Now we didn't really hold much store in any bloke who would put broken glass on top of a wall. Sure the bugger had to be off his rocker, setting bits of broken glass like a snare for us. We'd see who'd get snared, Mister Broken Bottle. Having had the patience to wait for the juicy little apples to grow to full, we reckoned we owned them anyway.

On the day when we decided to collect, the formula was simple. The survival kit was made up of an old heavy chain and a brick. So much for most of the so-and-so glass. A few swipes and the pathway was clear. A couple of wipes with the chain and sure what was left we needed to hold a mat in place.

The best part was to come. We'd nip around to the front and grab the mat from outside the hall door and go down three or four houses and swap the mats. Now, armed with the neighbour's mat, put it nice and firmly on the spot on the wall we'd tidied up. Next move was to call around to the front door and knock like hell. When Mr Snareglass or Mrs Snareglass appeared, simply tell them there's a fellah robbing mats from one house and selling them to the next. 'Sure didn't I see him meself? He took the very mat out of this porch and went two doors down and sold it.'

Sweet Jesus, the house would be in an uproar and all the Snareglasses would be out. You know the type yourself.

Meanwhile the mates were working like Billio out the back. Next move was to get the Snareglasses down to view their mat outside the neighbour's. Now this could go a few ways. First if he knocked and there was nobody in, you'd swear blind there was five minutes ago and maybe they were afraid to open the door. Suspicion all around from the Snareglasses. Jasus, they even had a witness – me – 'receiving stolen property' and all would come out. Whatever happened to love thy neighbour?

If the door was opened, you'd let Mr Snareglass do all the talking, sure he looked and sounded like the gobshite he was. Just stay out of arm's reach and nothing between you and the gate. By the time the oul' Snareglasses started to blurt out the great wrong done on their lot, the door would usually be slammed in their faces, and Mr Snareglass would reach down and grab the mat with great dignity and strut back home, his pride intact, if not his marbles.

One thing was for sure, his apples were far from intact. They were halfway to the Drive. And I often got a reward of thrupence or sixpence for doing my civic duty. Now on to the divvy-up in the field and the next target. Stash the apples and break our hearts laughing. We could just imagine them going out the back, and seein' the neighbour's mat on the wall and the trees bare, and them having maybe given a reward for being done. Well, what did they expect? We just loved their apples a little more than they loved their neighbour. Weren't we only doing the same thing as oul' Adam, only better?

WHAT'S WHAT

In summer there'd be excursions to Dollier – or Dollymount Strand. Watch out for Peggy's Hole, the Red Flag, the timber bridge. Sand in your sandwiches and everywhere else. Jasus, you'd be tired by the time you got far enough out to swim. Half Dublin there on a half-decent day. The learner drivers, the mad drivers – no speed limit.

Still, Dollier was better than the other choices of Bray or Rush. Bray with its Esplanade, as the oul' fellah'd say. The Ma never seemed to be able to pronounce the word so she called it 'the Prom'. We'd all be done out in our best gear and start the march at the harbour end. If the oul' fellah told me once he told me a thousand times, 'See the end of that pier? Well, that's where the lighthouse fell into the sea.' He even brought me up to see it. He thought it was a bigger event than the *Titanic* goin' down.

At the start of our walk we'd see all the dealers selling their cockles and mussels, jellied eels in jars, periwinkles, oysters, shrimps and prawns and all the English holidaymakers who were over for the cheap beer and smokes queuing up to sample the seafood delights.

We couldn't afford them, so on off with us past them and the kiosks as though they were invisible. Ice cream was only for the tourists. Past the amusements as they were only for gobshites. The only possible stop'd be for either the jacks, or the band stands where we'd watch the Irish dancing or listen to the brass bands or the Irish pipe bands decked out in their kilts and all. The holidaymakers'd rent out deckchairs to sit around. Jasus, they had to be daft, didn't they know the ground was free?

Off with us right up to the end of the Prom to the Escalator. Now if we'd made it up that far without sweets, ice cream, amusements and paddle-boats this was our prize – a trip up in the Escalator. To hop into your chair and be whisked off up to the heavens was a real thrill. Just close your eyes and imagine you were goin' up Mount Everest.

I hated goin' up with the brod 'cause he used to spit at the cars coming down. More than once he had me bleeding terrified goin' to throw me out. Or else he'd start tellin' me how old the Jasus thing was. Swear he'd heard a strand of wire snap.

I got the better o' him though 'cause the Da told him to mind me. So naturally when we were three-quarters the way up I tell him I reckon I can jump and make it the way they do in the flicks. He sneers at me. Well, fuck him. When he isn't looking out I go. Mind you, it was only about twenty feet down, stupid no way. Sure the minute I jumped some bollocks stopped the lift and it stayed stopped till I walked back down to the Da. He hugged and squeezed me and thanked God. The Ma was havin' none of that and gave me what for there and then. Jasus, there was consternation and the brod was in big shit. So was fucking I, not a scratch or sprain from the jump, but black and blue from the Ma. All o' Bray seemed to know about my jump, fingers pointing everywhere I looked.

It was worth it to see the brod dangling there in his chair with his face as white as chalk. I knew I'd get a hiding but it shut him up. He wasn't the big shot put in charge o' me anymore after that, the oul' fellah took over.

A few years later the Escalator was shut down. I wondered if maybe the brod had been tellin' the truth, but consoled meself 'cause that'd be totally out o' character for him where I'm concerned.

Whenever we went to Rush we'd be in no hurry there. All day in the sand waitin' for the tide to go out. Then off over to the back pier to get periwinkles and catch crabs. The same oul' bands and dancers and nowhere to go but home if it rained. It was only an excuse for a day out.

What about the ferry that brought the dockers in and out to work across the Liffey and the Half Moon Club? Some bloke from far away from our bleedin' ferry down in Ringsend is singin' a song, 'Don't pay the ferryman till you get to the other side'. Easy know he wasn't one of our lot, since we never paid at all. That beautiful ferry going from side to side of our own Liffey and the crew, kindly oul' sorts, oul' Dubs, sure you'd know it a mile off.

Havin' passed over by Tara Street and down by the Port till we reached our own ferry boat, I used to close my eyes and think I was on board one of the Irish big ships with Dangerously Violent, the brod. The oul' fellah said a few years at sea'd sort him out. Lord love the oul' fellah, sure he'd to get him out o' jail in Japan and Canada one after the other and then out of the Merchant Navy fast.

I was sick and tired writing the brod to tell him what he was missin', and the Ma went mad when she read the letters I was gettin' back telling me what I was missin'. Sure I couldn't make head nor tail of it, but the oul' fellah could. Can still see me granny's face when I asked her for a short arm inspection and held out my two arms. She nearly died laughin'. Then when I asked the oul' fellah what jiggy jig was, he nearly had a stroke. 'Get down those letters o' yours now,' he says. Before he was halfway through the first one I knew there was trouble brewin'. Where does he go next but in to see the priest, then two or three hours go by and I'm not stupid so I know it's not the spellin' that's bein' corrected. Next I'm brought in and the Reverend Father asks me do I know the meaning o' this and that.

'If I knew I wouldn't be askin',' says I. Now I'm gettin' pissed off with all this cloak and dagger stuff, so I says, 'Do you know? And if you do, tell me and if you don't, sure I can bring them into school and get the master to work it out for me terrible simple.'

Back into our house, Da and me, and the oul' fellah keeps me letters. Refuses to talk about them. Never saw them since. Thanks be to Jasus the Da only got the brother's letters to me otherwise I'd've been banjaxed.

The ferry's gone, the water's polluted and the people don't talk anymore. Not much left to take away is there? The school around the corner nowadays may as well be in Hyde Park Corner and the kids are just drug bait and dole bait, but the system works. Ask any teacher or school manager or politician. But that's where it stops working. Statistics, that's the new word for sums and they show how well the system works for the teachers and managers. 'Fuck the kids, sure they're no concern of ours.' Points galore and they'll end up with pints galore. Don't you know education is big business, otherwise the clergy wouldn't be in it? Property, cash flow, politics, and pensions are what it's about now.

From coffin ships, to the EU or to America with a Morrison Visa. Same jump, same plight, that's progress. Real class. 'Love everyone, trust few, always paddle your own canoe, and make sure you stay away from the pros,' me granny used to say. Now, you might think that this meant stay out of Monto with the motts sitting in behind them halfdoors, but even as a kid I knew what she meant. Doctors, solicitors, dentists and undertakers. She maintained, as only me granny could, that if you went to any of them you'd be putting your life on the line. Sure going to a doctor and asking him for a check-up would make her laugh. Sweet Jesus, how many times could a doctor get you to call back, paying the half crown a go, for the flu? Wasn't it his bank manager that was calling you back, not your health?

As for solicitors, she saw less use for them. 'Do you think I have a case, Mr So-and-So?' Sure, sweet Jasus, 'Can I give you my money, Mr So-and-So?' The same as asking a beggar, 'Do you need the coppers?' Wasn't it the solicitor's job to convince you you'd been wronged? Afterwards you'd carry the can anyway because you'd be like a beggar after paying him.

Now when it came down to the dentists who scraped into the so-called professions, she'd say, 'Never get a filling, get the tooth out and keep their wives skinny, that way you'll get the full set sooner.' With regard to the undertakers she used to laugh: 'He'll get you anyway but it won't be your worry.' When it came down to the prostitutes, sure she'd say, 'Them poor girls,' and I always wondered what she was on about.

Whenever we saw them they had as much jewellery on them as the Queen, the very best of gear. This led me to believe that the Queen was the top dog brasser. Did you ever see as much jewellery, Coronation and all. Wasn't she doing all right? Me granny was always praying for them, so were me fuckin' brothers, I suspect for different reasons though.

Yes, towards the end of the fifties my innocence was going.

Kittens at home saw to that, along with the dogs in the street. The next thing would be some young one who was out robbing an orchard with you, or helping you make a gig a week or two ago appeared out in nylons, head high in the air and she wouldn't even look at you. 'Jasus, look at what happened to her,' we'd say, but in time it all fell into place.

Going from innocence caused many's the row as we were facing it from innocence. We were bewildered by those who had grown up, but in a sense this bewilderment could not be escaped. You're well out of it now, Granny, and the Queen and her lot have yet to change their line of work in spite of your prayers.

ONE + ONE = THREE

On one of me talks with the Da he asked me did I know how I 'came to bein'', as he put it. Mind you, this had been botherin' me as most of me mates had been delivered by the Coombe. 'Yeah,' I said. I was delivered by Dr Raymond Cross. I always felt special, a step up on the mates. What came next was natural – I'd seen the cat havin' kittens – but somewhere along the lines of the conversation I got confused.

First the Da tells me about the queen bee. She picks out the drone who flies up after her and she comes together with him. Then he's done in, dead like. Then it's over to the queen bee to raise the family. Jasus, you'd have to be some stupid class of a drone bee to go for that deal.

He asks me do I understand the penetration and consummation and planting of the seed. 'Yeah, I do, Da, for bees.' Well, he tells me to go to the Sodality on the sixth night and the priest will be tellin' all that's there the full story. 'Enough for now,' he says. Could you imagine dying for some scrubber queen bleedin' bee?

The Sodality came in due course. All I could hear was 'dultery calumniation wives tend to your husbands husbands tend to your wives'. Jasus, this fucker should be talkin' to bees!

For the full picture Gussie is the only one I trust. I felt a fool askin' him, knowin' well he'd more than likely tell me a pack o' lies. But I don't know what came over the brother – he must a passed a few churches that day 'cause he told me the truth.

I asked the Da, just to check on what the brother told me. He confirmed it all.

Why bother? I asked the Da. He said he often asked himself the same question when all came to all. But he held on to me and told me, me body'd tell me in its own good time.

I went back to Gussie and asked him why he told me the truth and when I'd know. The brother wants to know if I'm up to it. He wants to fix me up straight away for a trial run with a mott who owes him a favour. The brod has a reputation, as he put it, so it's now up to me. He reminds me of how I'd never let him down in a scrap, but that this was even more important.

When I tell Da the plan he fuckin' explodes and goes after the brother – all over bleedin' bees and birds, a mott and me.

THE LINGO

In the fifties, can you imagine explaining to my oul' fellah that two yellow lines meant you can't park here or your car will be towed off, he'd tell you to fuck off first. Or that you can't drive on the crown of the road and a drip line dictates whether you can pass out or not. Good Christ! 'Sure have we all lost our pride?' he'd have said.

In those days, currency was *lsd*. That meant pounds, shilling and pence as opposed to today's meaning – drugs! Acid was for cleaning drains and not your brains. Speed meant how fast you could move. Queer meant a bit off the head, a nice way of saying simple. Jet-lag and burn-out had yet to be invented, the radio was the keystone of entertainment. Then records and tape recorders along with fridges, telephones and televisions crept in slowly and invaded any code of silence which had survived. Cars appeared in driveways and HP was no longer sauce but Hire Purchase or the Never Never .

'It was easy to have the best car on the road,' my Da'd say, 'Just pay for it in cash.' If ever a man hated the hire purchase companies it was him. Just a step below the banks, he put it, and they're only a step away from slot machines. If someone suggested the drip when he was around you could count on a row.

The cost of living was simple for me, one penny bar, or twelve aniseed balls for one penny, or a twopenny wafer, or a thrupenny bar of chocolate, or fourpence for the new invention – Tayto crisps with the little bag of salt inside. A jam jar was worth one penny for a one pound jar and tuppence for a two pound jar. A mineral bottle was worth tuppence on return. Any of the luxuries I wanted would have to be financed this way. Swapping was the order of the day and the key to survival was always to have something that the other fellah wanted.

We were dragged away from the Crystal sets and gas mask games into a new dimension of immediate satisfaction or gratification. Fair dues to the Church, it did its bit to try to keep moneylenders, legal and not, out. But the lure of the luxuries always proved too much. How could we stand against the tide? The BBC decided world morality and that was that. You could say what you liked from the pulpit, Reverend, but your words only flowed out the doors like a pint of porter down Jimmy's throat. The only difference was that the porter gave results. Sodalities, processions, retreats, the Legion of Mary – good for a try but only worked on those at death's door. The ten Thou Shalt Nots started to be met with a 'Why should we travel to England to be free of them. Sure can't we be free here?'

As romantic as you may be led to believe it was back then, it wasn't. It stank like the putrid smell of O'Keeffe's, the knackers, and crept through Crumlin like a Guinness barge up the canal, man-made, virtually silent, the goods deep in the hold, giving the appearance of security in motion. This penetration could not be reversed. What was to follow? That was the question. Even had we known the consequences we could never have repelled the invasion. A nation divided once again and again and again and again.

ENOUGH!

What I have tried to set out here is the reality of life in Dublin in the fifties where if you saw someone wearing an anorak it meant he had relations in the States who had sent home their cast-offs.

Kindness and security went hand in hand. No matter where you were in our town, cry help and help was there. Cry loneliness and company was there. Cry, and it was heard by one and all, to be responded to with love. What I decry are the tools of modernisation which stifled this cry. It's easy to be angry. As with the stifled cry, we were doomed to the loss of security, comfort and love. Pride would be the ally as of now and we would have to learn to close our hearts. A cry became an evil, and then we'd learn to bring it a stage further. Hear no evil, see no evil, speak no evil. Yes, we would have to move away from what our hearts told us, to a new way of dealing with our reality.

Laughter became a smirk, kindness became weakness, and those with both would learn to hide both. We would be doomed to sit in buses not talking to one another one-upmanship now being the basis of life. Is this living? I don't think so. Our town became a city. What an achievement and what a price.

There are at least one hundred stories I could tell of growing up in my town but to what end? All they could say is, 'You can't do that nowadays because ...' A great man said, 'Our revels now are ended,' and so it is with the Dub. It was silent, and we learned to be silenced. To stand up and be counted is a losing proposition. Your family will be targeted and when your strength is spent, or wisdom twisted to suit others, what of you?

When you're down, down y'are.

We all make mistakes and it's easy to love a memory, just as I often romanticise about the horns going off in the morning to get the workers into Wills's or Jacob's. Sure some days the smell would waft up from either factory and it was the best ad either could ever have had. The Wills's smell of tobacco, sweet with a cutting edge, a pure perfume for Crumlin. The Jacob's bakery smell that told you it was time to get the broken biscuits. The trouble with this romanticising is that you forget the queues outside the pawnshop on a Monday of fifty or sixty people standing in the cold and rain in their prison of indignity, gaunt, desperate for a way out. Cromwell in his day said, 'To Hell or to Connaught'. Now the cry was, 'Out by boat or pine from our own again'. Haven't we come a long ways all the same? Nowadays the cry is, 'Out by boat or *plane* or pine'. Small wonder we opened our hearts to the boat people in recent years, sure we were the same.

Our main export is human beings, ask the clergy about the hidden political truths. Haven't we supplied Britain with navvies and prostitutes for eight hundred years? The air travel, however, adds a certain dignity to it, especially if you go from Knock. Doesn't it make sense really? Sure we're only the Irish. To compound or confuse the issue let's see it as it is.

Pine, boat or plane for each parent's loving, sacred trust of beautiful children to be ravished further afield in Europe. Sure they'll find it easier to hide the indignity of their plight as the distance will cloak them. But this plight is silent and unceasing, not like the honesty of the blight on the humble potato. Sure we'll hear from the Dáil that it's really down to the weather! I say it's whether they live up to their responsibilities or whether they don't. No pockets in the shroud, but what dignity will these pillars of society have to present their maker with?

These examples of happenings in the fifties, while simple, shouldn't be scorned. We lived, we had hope, we had one another, we had dignity, we had loyalty, we had compassion. We were what and who we were. Try it today and the city will eat you up. Howth to Bray you were safe as a child. Those slightly touched were part of us and not incarcerated in asylums to suit the dignity of those with power, for fear they would be embarrassed by them. It is far from their safety the true issue is. It just doesn't look good to the tourists. Well, it doesn't look too fucking good for us now, Mr Petfood Man.

Yes, our town was broken up and conquered but that's only a battle lost, the best is yet to come, when the sick, the young and the unemployed, those suffering forced indignity, cry 'Enough!' Where will you run to hide, you men with little faith in your fellow Irishmen, when the capital of Ireland rejects you and your broken promises to the defenceless ones? Yes, we learned from Brendan Behan to look down on you from the gutter, but now we'll bring you down. Curse as only a Dub can on your issue and await the day when we say together 'Enough! No more,' and, to conclude, the victory will fall to us. We've had enough of 'Alas, poor Yorick'. All men don't kill the thing they love.

There was a crooked man, but now there are many.